102

Fascinating

Bible Studies

102

Fascinating

Bible Studies

Preston A. Taylor

BETHANYHOUSE
MINNEAPOLIS, MINNESOTA

Published by Bethany House Publishers
11400 Hampshire Avenue South
Bloomington, Minnesota 55438

Bethany House Publishers is a division of
Baker Publishing Group, Grand Rapids, Michigan.

Printed in the United States of America

Library of Congress Cataloging-in-Publication Data

Taylor, Preston A.
    102 fascinating Bible studies : for personal or small group use / Preston A. Taylor.
      p. cm.
    Includes bibliographical references.
    Summary: "A retired pastor and missionary provides a collection of brief topical Bible studies for small groups or personal study"—Provided by publisher.
    ISBN 978-0-7642-0837-9 (pbk. : alk. paper) 1. Bible—Textbooks. I. Title. II. Title: One hundred two fascinating Bible studies for personal or small group use.
    BS605.3T39   2010
    220.071—dc22

2010014543

In keeping with biblical principles of creation stewardship, Baker Publishing Group advocates the responsible use of our natural resources. As a member of the Green Press Initiative, our company uses recycled paper when possible. The text paper of this book is comprised of 30% post-consumer waste.

green press
INITIATIVE

Dedicated to Preston Jr. and Marsha Kay
and
to the churches where I have had
the privilege of serving
and
to God's eternal cause, worldwide.

Blessings to all,

PRESTON A. TAYLOR

BIBLE STUDY
TOPICS

A Practical Plan for Topical Bible Study

Welcome to an exciting Bible adventure. The goal of *102 Fascinating Bible Studies* is to do three things: (1) get readers more interested in the Bible as they search the Scriptures on each topic; (2) provide a unique and unparalleled resource for devotional or group Bible studies; and (3) give everyone the opportunity to have refreshing fellowship with others.

If you are using this book with a small group, let me make a few suggestions. These are not hard and fast rules, but simply things I have learned over decades of leading Bible studies.

It would be best if each participant had a Bible and a copy of this book for study and sharing. The group leader should give each person time to locate every Scripture. No one should feel intimidated or embarrassed about not knowing where some books of the Bible are located. Genesis, Matthew, and Revelation may be easy to find, but most of us have a limited knowledge of the Bible, so help each other out and have fun locating the various books. Also, some may not remember how to spell or pronounce the names of some of the minor prophets or which book comes before another. The same difficulty arises with some New Testament books. Who doesn't have a rather quizzical look when a few Bible books are mentioned: Nahum, Habakkuk, Zechariah, Jude?

In following this topical study, we go from Genesis to Revelation. That is, the Old and New Testament references go in orderly progression within every topic. The sessions will be more effective if everyone reviews the topic to be discussed before the group meets. Spiritual insights will electrify your group as you get together and talk about God and His matchless Book, the Bible.

Ten Bible verses are listed in each unit. The group should take the time to thoroughly explore each topic, even if this means two sessions for a particular theme. When any group reaches fifteen members, it may be wise to form another group so that every person will have an opportunity to participate. Try to control the time for discussion, whether you have decided on thirty- or forty-five-minute sessions. Rarely should the study time last more than one hour. Remember, you will meet again, and respecting a scheduled time will lead to continued participation.

More than one thousand Scripture references are included in this book. The advantages of this study depend partly upon a review of the Bible verses *and their context* before the group meets (especially the leader). The Question and Answer (Q & A) plan is simple to use anytime. A PowerPoint presentation could also be used or some other approach the group might prefer.

The leader of a group may invite others to lead or team teach. One of the benefits of this book is that it is not hard to use for even a novice Bible study leader. Everyone should be reminded that they have the freedom to ask questions, make comments, and discuss the topics at length. The study is not intended to be a lecture or a one-man show.

Our prayer is that God will bless you as you journey through these provocative topics that we hope will keep you turning the pages of the Bible. As you begin each session, ask God to bless the time spent in fellowship and in His Word.

This book is not only for small groups. You may be an individual who is simply looking for a little more diversity in your daily time with the Lord and Scripture. Hopefully this book can provide you with a refreshing alternative to your normal routine. However you use this book, may God bless your time in His Word.

—Preston A. Taylor

Amen

1

We end our prayers with *Amen*, which means "Let it be so." The expression gives strong approval to what has been said or done. In some churches, years ago, a group of men would sit in a special area called the "Amen corner." When the preacher said things they liked, or particularly agreed with, they would say *Amen*.

The Bible uses the word *amen* more than seventy times. Sometimes it is used when people act in a way that God approves, such as when a crowd shouts *Amen* when someone speaks a spiritual truth. On the other hand, it is also used when evil people hear a warning about the dangers of doing wrong. When God provides good things for His people, we can say *Amen*.

Frequently in the Scriptures, both men and women say *Amen*. Where the Spirit of the Lord is, we have freedom to express ourselves. Look at this limited selection of Scriptures where this word is used:

1. Deuteronomy 27:15. An *Amen* is spoken after a commandment that idol worshipers will suffer. Why? Can a person have fellowship or a relationship with idols?

2. Nehemiah 8:1–6. Where were the people when Ezra read from the Book of the Law? What did they do when he finished reading? What did the *Amen* mean?

3. Psalm 89:52. Why does this verse use the word *amen* two times? Read the preceding verses 1, 6, 8, and 15–16, which will help explain why the chapter ends with a double *amen.*

4. Romans 9:4–5. What advantages did the Jewish nation have in the Old Testament? Who came from that nation? Why is an *Amen* said here?

5. 2 Corinthians 1:19–20. What affirmations do we give about Jesus, the Son of God? What is said about God's promises in Christ? Who should say *Amen?*

6. Galatians 1:3–5. What has Christ done for us? What double blessings come our way because of Jesus? Why should one respond with an affirmation of these truths?

7. 2 Timothy 4:14–18. When Paul had no defenders, who came to his rescue? Who was the "lion" that wanted to kill Paul? Why did Paul say *Amen?*

8. 2 Peter 3:18. How can a person have a growing relationship with Jesus our Lord and Savior? How long does glory belong to Jesus? Why is there an *Amen* in this verse?

9. Revelation 5:13–14. What do you think of the hymn of praise to Jesus in verse 13? Who sang it? What do you think of the *Amen* in this text?

10. Revelation 22:20–21. Why should an *Amen* be given when Jesus testified about the truths of Revelation? Why does God's grace merit an *Amen?*

Angels

2

The word *angel* means "messenger." Angels are supernatural beings that serve God and man, and the Bible refers to them about two hundred times. When angels are visible they look like ordinary men (Hebrews 13:2). The Pharisees of New Testament times believed angels existed; the Sadducees did not. Do you? Let's spend some time talking about and discussing God's angels. (See any Bible dictionary or view the bibliography at the end of this book for further reading about angels as well as any of the other topics.)

1. Psalm 34:7. What does the statement mean that the angel of the Lord surrounds those who fear Him? If you saw an angel, how do you think you might react?

2. Daniel 6:21–22. How did an angel help Daniel? Discuss the story. When do you believe angels may intervene in our lives today? How and why?

3. Matthew 4:11. After Christ fasted forty days, why do you think angels ministered to Him? What do you think they did for Jesus?

4. Luke 15:8–10. Do angels have an interest in a person's salvation?

How did the woman react when she found her money? What lessons does this parable teach?

5. Luke 16:19–22. Where was Lazarus, the poor man? What happened to him? Do you think angels might have an ongoing ministry to dying believers?

6. John 20:1, 10–13. How many angels sat in Christ's empty tomb? What did they do and say? How did the angels illustrate their strength and agility?

7. Acts 5:17–24. How did an angel help the apostles who had been sent to prison by Jewish leaders? What did an angel tell the apostles to do?

8. Hebrews 1:14. How are angels described in this verse? Who do angels sometimes serve? What did an angel do for Elijah (1 Kings 19:3–8)?

9. Hebrews 12:22–24. What does the verse mean about angels being in joyful assembly? Do we have any idea about the number of angels God created (Revelation 5:11)?

10. Revelation 19:10. What reaction did John have to an angel who appeared to him on the Isle of Patmos? How did the angel describe himself?

Anger or Wrath

Jonathan Edwards (1703–1758) entered Yale College at thirteen years of age, graduating four years later at the head of his class. Edwards served as the third president of Yale. His fame lives on because of his leadership during the revivals or what was known as the Great Awakening in New England. His most famous sermon was titled "Sinners in the Hands of an Angry God." Do we tend to deny or not teach the truth of God's wrath in our day?

Most everyone becomes angry at one time or another, and if we allow anger to expand, we may call it wrath. We usually attach a negative meaning to anger or wrath, but these emotions take place in almost everyone's life. The range of anger is as broad as life's experiences. Let's look at some Scriptures that relate to the topic of anger or wrath.

1. Genesis 4:1–8. Who were Adam and Eve's first two sons? Why did Cain become angry with his brother? What did he do? Why is anger potentially dangerous?

2. Exodus 4:10–17. Why did God become angry with Moses? Can God become upset with people who offer excuses or who should serve Him, but don't? To what extent? (See Isaiah 57:16.)

3. 2 Kings 5:10–14. What reaction did Naaman have to Elisha's

message? How did Naaman's servants handle the situation? What would you do in such a crisis?

4. Mark 3:1–6. What did Jesus do that caused the religious leaders to become angry with Him? What reaction did Jesus have to His critics? When is anger the correct response?

5. John 3:35–36. What calamity will people suffer who reject Jesus as God's Son and only world Redeemer? What is your definition of God's wrath?

6. Romans 1:18–27. Why is God's wrath against those who practice immorality? Can we affirm those who continue in a sinful life style? Why or why not?

7. James 1:19–20. Why and when do we sometimes become angry too quickly? What are some ways we can put the brakes on anger?

8. Revelation 6:15–17. What action will all kinds of unbelievers take when Christ comes again? Why will they become fearful of God's wrath?

9. Revelation 12:12, 17. Why is the devil enraged? How and against whom is Satan displaying his rage? What is our refuge against Satan's attacks? (Isaiah 59:19; Matthew 4:1–4).

10. Revelation 19:15–26. How will Jesus finally express God's wrath against all those who approve of evil and oppose God and His eternal truth?

Antichrist—
the Man of Sin

During Joseph Stalin's teenage years he attended a Catholic seminary in Russia, but when he was nineteen, the seminary expelled him because of his revolutionary activities. Authorities sent Stalin into Siberian exile, but he escaped and joined Lenin's Communist party in 1917. He succeeded Lenin in 1924, and during his thirty-year rule, Stalin and his forces killed approximately 30 million people. In those years, some called Stalin the Antichrist.

The Bible reveals very little about the final Antichrist who seemingly will head up the government of the world near history's end. Roman emperors and other leaders across the centuries have been called the Antichrist. However, no one really knows all about the Antichrist, including religious gurus. Let's view some Scriptures that reveal some truths about antichrists and the final Antichrist.

1. Exodus 7:8–13. Egypt's magicians may have been a type, or symbol, of the Antichrist. How did Pharaoh's puppets mimic some of God's miracles and oppose the God of Israel?

2. Daniel 7:19–28. Who does the eleventh horn represent? What havoc does he cause? Who comes to rescue the saints? Who has the victory? What is Daniel's reaction to this vision?

3. Daniel 8:9–27. What did the "other horn" do? What being appears near the end of his reign? What will he do? Did Daniel understand all of the vision? Can we?

4. Daniel 11:36–39. What will the mysterious king do for himself and others? What kind of success will he have? Until what time will he have success?

5. Matthew 24:15–25. Daniel wrote about "the abomination that causes desolation," referred to here in Daniel 9:27. What will the false prophets and false Christs do? (See the warning in John 5:43.)

6. 2 Thessalonians 2:3–4. Who is the "man of lawlessness," the "man doomed to destruction"? When will he appear? What work will the final Antichrist do in God's temple or church?

7. 2 Thessalonians 2:5–12. Who has victory over the Antichrist? What kind of work will he be doing? How is Satan involved? What happens to the deluded?

8. 1 John 2:18–23. What does this verse say about antichrists? What does the word *antichrist* mean? What does an antichrist say about Jesus and God?

9. 1 John 4:1–3; 2 John 1:7. How can you identify the spirit of antichrist? What does the second reference say about those who deny that Christ has come in the flesh?

10. Revelation 13:1–10. Where does this Antichrist get his power? Who does he slander? Who will worship the Antichrist? What action do God's saints take?

Baptism

5

I made my profession of faith during a revival, or evangelistic meeting. That night I tried to tell some boys in a clumsy way that my heart felt spiritually warmed. The following Sunday afternoon the pastor baptized me and several others in a lake in that community. Can you share your baptismal experience?

The New Testament gives several accounts of people who were baptized. Baptism in that era followed a person's confession of faith in Jesus Christ as Savior. Of course, the thief on the cross made his repentance and confession to Jesus, but had no opportunity to express that faith through baptism. We don't all agree on the details of baptism, but it is called a New Testament ordinance, or sacrament, by some. Let's look at some Scripture references about baptism.

1. Matthew 3:1–10. Describe John the Baptist. What did he demand of those who wanted to be baptized by him in the Jordan River? Who should be baptized?

2. Matthew 3:13–17. Who baptized Jesus? Why was He baptized? What two events took place when Christ was baptized?

3. Matthew 28:18–20. What instructions did the apostles hear from

Jesus before He ascended to heaven? What specifically is involved in the Great Commission?

4. John 4:1–2. What rumor circulated at that time? Why do you think Jesus did not baptize His followers? Why do you think Jesus gained more disciples than John?

5. Acts 2:38. What did Peter tell the Jewish converts to do? What gift would they receive? Does baptism save a person? Was the thief on the cross baptized?

6. Acts 9:1–20. What happened to Paul as he came near Damascus? Who was sent to help Paul in Damascus? What did Ananias tell Paul?

7. Acts 10:45–78. Who received the gift of the Holy Spirit when Peter preached? What did the Gentiles do when they believed? Biblically, who should be baptized?

8. Acts 16:11–15. Who did Paul and his friends meet beside a river outside of Philippi? What did that family do when they heard the message of Christ?

9. 1 Corinthians 12:13. Paul wrote about spiritual baptism. Who baptizes believers into one body? What is that body? What does it mean to drink of one Spirit?

10. 1 Corinthians 15:29. What do you think this verse means? Baptism by proxy is a false teaching, with no examples of the doctrine of baptism for the dead in the Bible.

Beatitudes

6

Children love to receive Christmas presents, birthday presents, gifts at the end of school, and any other time. Most all of us like to receive good presents, don't we? Jesus talked about the gift of blessing in His Sermon on the Mount.

What kind of blessings would you like to receive from the Lord? Have you thought of blessings that you could give or share with others? Before beginning an exploration of the Beatitudes that introduce Jesus' Sermon on the Mount, let's consider briefly their background.

1. Matthew 3:1–4:25. What major events took place in the life and ministry of Jesus immediately before the Sermon on the Mount?

2. Matthew 5:1–2. Gleaning from the previous verses, about how many people heard the Sermon on the Mount? Where was Jesus at the time? What did Jesus do as He started to teach? Why do you think He did so?

3. Matthew 5:3. Who are the poor in spirit that Jesus speaks of? Are they proud and haughty or spiritually empty and destitute? Describe what you think it means. What is their reward?

4. Matthew 5:4. Those who mourn may refer to those who have sorrow over their spiritually bankrupt condition. How are they continually comforted?

5. Matthew 5:5. Who are the meek? Jesus taught that meekness is submission to God, not weakness. What do the meek inherit? (See 1 Corinthians 3:21–22.)

6. Matthew 5:6. What does it mean to hunger and thirst for righteousness? What does it mean to be filled? Why do some love backsliding more than right living?

7. Matthew 5:7. Who are the merciful? How can we show kindness and mercy toward those who are downcast or miserable? Why do we want God to be merciful to us?

8. Matthew 5:8. Who are the pure in heart? Is this righteousness self-attained or is it the result of being rightly related to Jesus? What does it mean to see God?

9. Matthew 5:9. Do you think most people are in the peace-breakers or peacemakers camp? How can nations become peacemakers? What are peacemakers called?

10. Matthew 5:10–12. Name some Bible people who were persecuted for believing in God (Hebrews 11). Can you name some contemporary people who have been persecuted? What are some rewards of persecution?

Bible—
the Scriptures

7

President George Washington said, "It is impossible to rightly govern the world without God and the Bible" (*Halley's Bible Handbook*, 18). The word *Bible* means "book." The Bible is made up of the Old and New Testaments, the Old Testament containing thirty-nine books, and the New Testament twenty-seven. God's Word was written by about forty men over a period of 1,500 years, from the time of Moses until John the apostle wrote the book of Revelation. God's Word is complete. The Bible is the greatest book ever written, and there will never be an equal to it. Notice some important truths about the Bible:

1. Joshua 1:8–9. Where should God's Word be? When and how do we meditate on His Word? What happens to those who do what this Scripture instructs us to do?

2. 2 Chronicles 34:1–33. Where did Hilkiah find God's Word (vv. 14–16)? What response did King Josiah make (vv. 31–33)? How might we lose or find the Bible today?

3. Psalm 119:11, 105, 130. How does the Bible keep us from sin? How does it give light for our path? How does the Bible give understanding?

4. Isaiah 40:8. Most books have a short shelf life. Grass withers. Flowers fade and lose their beauty. What did Isaiah say about God's Word? Tell how this is a proven fact.

5. Jeremiah 15:16; 23:29. What happened when Jeremiah "ate" God's Word? To what did he compare God's Word? How is the Bible like a hammer?

6. Colossians 3:15–17. What does it mean to have God's Word living in us? How does the Bible challenge us to live? Why is the Bible the greatest book ever written?

7. 2 Timothy 3:15–17. What does verse 16 specifically teach about inspiration? In what ways is the Bible beneficial to us?

8. Hebrews 4:12. How do we know that the Bible is alive? How is the sharpness of the Bible described? What analysis does the Bible make of one's life?

9. 1 Peter 2:1–3. When should a new Christian begin to read the Bible? What does it mean to crave pure spiritual milk, or earnestly desire the Scriptures? Why should we desire God's Word?

10. 2 Peter 1:19–21. How did the Old Testament prophets speak God's message? How did the Holy Spirit make possible their proclamation? How is the Bible made effective in us?

Blind or Blindness

8

Helen Keller became blind and deaf at the age of two. However, she graduated from Radcliffe College with honors and became a champion of the blind and deaf. To lack physical sight is obviously a critical problem. Many vision-impaired people have learned Braille, and some use white canes or have service dogs to help them get around. But even with these tools, the Helen Kellers of this world face difficulties that most of us will never know or understand.

The Bible also mentions spiritual blindness. To suffer a lack of spiritual sight is even more critical than the lack of physical sight. Spiritual blindness places people on the "endangered species" list, and these people often cry out to us for help. Are we ready to help the blind see what God has for all who have their eyes open to His grace and love? Let's look at the problem of physical and spiritual blindness from the biblical perspective.

1. Job 29:14–16. When Job's friends criticized him, he said that he helped the blind and the lame. What did Job mean by these words? How can we imitate Job?

2. Isaiah 59:10. Isaiah described those without spiritual vision as people who grope for walls, stumble at midday, and act like dead men. How is this true today?

3. Matthew 15:14. What did Jesus mean when He said that some leaders are like the blind who lead the blind? What happens to these leaders and the ones they lead?

4. Matthew 23:24. Jesus faced critical religious leaders. What did He say about them and how do we interpret and apply His words about gnats and camels?

5. Mark 10:46–52. What kind of a crowd met Jesus in Jericho? As He left the city, who asked for mercy? What did Jesus do? What "blind spots" do we have?

6. Acts 13:6–12. When Paul and Barnabas arrived on the island of Cyprus, they witnessed to the governor, Sergius Paulus. Who opposed them? What did Paul do?

7. 2 Corinthians 3:14. Paul said the Israelites had a veil over their minds. What did he mean by that statement? How has Christ made it possible for the blind to see?

8. 2 Corinthians 4:4. How does Satan blind people to the truth of Jesus? What is the effect of being blind to the gospel? What can we do for the spiritually blind?

9. Romans 11:23–26. What has happened in part to the Jewish nation? What advantage has this given to the Gentiles? What does it mean that all Israel will be saved?

10. 1 John 2:11. If a believer hates a fellow Christian, where is he walking? Does he know where he is going? What action should he take so that he might see?

Blood

Mel Gibson produced *The Passion of the Christ*, one of the most viewed films of all time. Millions of people sat in awe, and shock, as they witnessed the condemnation and beating that Christ endured before His death on the cross. The sacrificial death of Christ for humankind's redemption should be the number one news story in every country of the world. Let's look at the references relating to Christ's death and the blood He shed so that anyone might experience salvation and life eternal.

1. Exodus 12:13. Before Israel left Egypt, they sprinkled blood on the doorposts of their houses so the death angel would pass over them. What did that act symbolize that would happen thousands of years later?

2. Leviticus 17:11. The blood sprinkled on the altar in the tabernacle prefigured that Christ's blood would be shed for man's pardon. What else does this verse state?

3. Matthew 26:28. As Jesus instituted the Lord's Supper, what did the fruit of the vine symbolize? What is the benefit for those who believe in Christ's sacrificial blood?

4. Acts 20:28. What does it mean that the church is purchased with the blood of Jesus? Is there a way to buy salvation or have salvation by works? Why or why not?

5. Romans 3:23–26. How can sinful people be made right with God? How does faith in Christ's blood show that God is just while He also justifies those who believe?

6. Hebrews 9:14. How or by whom did Jesus offer His blood as a sacrifice to God? What two results does the blood of Christ give to the believer?

7. 1 Peter 1:18–19. What is not able to redeem a person? How is the blood of Christ described? What does it mean that there was no blemish in Christ's sacrifice?

8. 1 John 1:7. What benefits do Christians have for walking in spiritual light? What will Christ's blood do for believers? What sins can be cleansed by Christ's blood?

9. Revelation 1:5. Christ is God's faithful witness who came alive after His crucifixion. What other title does He have? Why is Christ the *only* sin bearer?

10. Revelation 7:14; 12:11. How do those who go through tribulation as well as everyone else have white robes? What are the avenues to victory?

Bold or Boldness

A giant named Goliath once stood on a battlefield before thousands of Israelite soldiers. That Philistine giant dared any Israelite to come out and fight him. The Hebrew soldiers shook with fear every day for forty days when the Philistine strolled out before them and roared out his challenge. Then one day the shepherd boy David appeared on the scene. He asked why everyone was afraid of Goliath. Soon David was rushing out to meet the enemy with his sling and five small stones, saying that he would face Goliath in the name of the Lord God of Israel. He hurled one stone at the giant, hitting him in the forehead, and the giant fell to the earth (see 1 Samuel 17). David was not afraid of a lion or a bear, nor was he afraid of the wicked giant. What about our boldness for the Lord? Are we filled with courage, or does fear hold us in its grip? If we are bold for the Lord, we will have freedom to speak words of wisdom in His name. Do you think most Christians are bold today? Look at what the Bible says about being bold in the Lord:

1. Proverbs 28:1. Who are the righteous and how can they express spiritual boldness? How can we be as bold as a lion? Why should believers be bold in today's world?

2. Mark 15:43. What does this verse say about Joseph? Why did he

go to Pilate? Did that act take courage on the part of the man from Arimathea? Why?

3. John 7:25–32. What did religious leaders want to do with Jesus? How did Jesus show that He was not afraid of them? Are we sometimes afraid to express boldness for Christ?

4. Acts 4:13. How did the crowd describe Peter and John? What special characteristic did the two apostles have? What gives God's people boldness?

5. Acts 4:31. Review the background of this Scripture. What two great events happened when believers prayed? Why are some of us timid rather than bold?

6. Acts 9:29; 14:3; 19:8. Who did Paul confront with the message of Jesus? What did some want to do to him? How did Paul respond?

7. Ephesians 3:12. What are some resources of spiritual boldness? Do you and I have confidence and freedom to talk to the Lord? Why or why not?

8. Ephesians 6:19–20. Why did Paul ask the saints of Ephesus to pray for him? Should we ask others to pray for us? Why did Paul want to be filled with boldness?

9. Hebrews 4:16. Do we have the authority and freedom to go into God's presence and speak with Him? Why or why not? What is the result of a bold approach in prayer?

10. 1 John 4:17. Why do people need boldness as they face the final day of judgment? What helps us to become bold and not afraid of the future?

Cheer or Encourage

Cheerleaders are a part of many sporting events. They play a big role in the enthusiasm of the fans as well as the teams. Churches need cheerleaders, too. Pastors, teachers, ushers, everyone appreciates a pat on the back or a word of appreciation for what they do. As followers of Jesus Christ, we should encourage others whenever we can and avoid negative thoughts and comments as much as possible.

Teachers, parents, pastors, every Christian should be in the business of encouraging others. Since the Lord cheers us along our pilgrim route, let's encourage someone every day.

1. Deuteronomy 24:5. In Old Testament days, when an Israelite man married, he was excused from military and other duties for one year to stay home and cheer his bride. How can we bring happiness and encouragement to our families?

2. Judges 9:13. In answer to the request of trees to rule over them, the vine said its duty was to make wine to cheer the gods and men. How might our actions cheer others?

3. Proverbs 15:13; 17:22. How can a happy heart animate you and produce good health like medicine? How can one's attitude crush the spirit and dry up the bones?

4. Ecclesiastes 11:9. Under what circumstances can it be wrong to have a cheerful life? If a person finds cheer and thrills in sinful living, what will God do?

5. Isaiah 41:6–7. Isaiah wrote that everyone said to his neighbor, "Be of good cheer, or be strong." How can we encourage our children, parents, church friends, and co-workers?

6. Zechariah 8:19. Sad fasts became joyful events in Israel. Why did God's people find these occasions to be glad?

7. Matthew 9:2. One day some men carried a paralytic to Jesus. Seeing their faith, He told the sick man to be of good cheer because his sins were forgiven. Discuss and apply this story.

8. Matthew 14:27. In the midst of a storm, Jesus told His disciples to be of good cheer. How can we take courage and not be afraid during stormy times and help others who face problems as well?

9. John 16:33. Why did Jesus tell His disciples to take heart, even though they would face tough times? Who needs to hear a hopeful word from you today?

10. Acts 27:23–25, 36. Looking at the context, where was Paul at this time? Who did Paul see and what was he told? Share experiences you may have had similar to this.

Children

Someone asked Susanna Wesley, the mother of John and Charles Wesley, how she was able to raise these two sons as she did. She told them it was by getting a firm grip on their hearts when they were young and never turning them loose. Susanna and her pastor husband had nineteen children, and all who lived to adulthood became Christians. Children need the love of their father and mother. They need a good education as well as spiritual instruction—Sunday school, Vacation Bible School, church camps; and the list goes on. When we think of raising children, let's keep in mind that the Bible is the perfect guidebook. Proverbs is a great prescription for child-rearing. When we stay with God's Book, we have the help that every family needs and we become the channels through which godly help continues to flow to our children. Are we prepared for the discipline of raising godly children?

1. Exodus 2:6–7. Refresh your mind on the story of the birth of Moses. What did his parents do for his welfare? What can we do to protect our children in evil times?

2. Deuteronomy 6:6–9. When is the best time to read the Bible with children, pray, and talk with them about how God wants your family to live and honor Him?

3. 1 Samuel 2:22–25. Why do you think Eli's two sons became immoral? What early training can parents give children that will help them live for Christ's glory?

4. Proverbs 4:1–27. This entire chapter presents the potential for rich blessings to be upon our children. Select a few verses to share and explain to your children.

5. Proverbs 22:6. What does it mean to train up a child? How much time should be given to children's training? How can we help children plan for the future?

6. Matthew 10:21. What causes some children to betray their parents? Why do some children rebel? Is the environment responsible for the behavior of our youth?

7. Mark 10:13–16. What attitude did the disciples have about children? What response did Jesus make regarding this attitude? Talk about how Jesus received the children.

8. Luke 11:11–13. Name some bad gifts that children could receive from parents. What good gifts should children receive? What does God as our loving parent provide?

9. Ephesians 6:1–4; Colossians 3:20. What promises are given to children who obey their parents? How does God feel about children who obey their parents?

10. 2 Timothy 3:14–15. When should children be taught the Scriptures? (Deuteronomy 6:6–9). How important is it to teach our children the Word of God?

Church

When people see a church building, the normal response is, "That's the First Assembly of God Church," "That's St. Mary's Catholic Church," "That's the First Methodist Church," or "That's Pine Ridge Baptist Church." We identify churches by denomination, but we know that neither these names nor the buildings compose the true church. The church is God's people. The Greek word for church is *ecclesia,* which means "the called out ones." That is, those whose lives have been transformed by the Holy Spirit and who gather to worship in Christ's name make up the body of Christ, including all the redeemed who might not have the privilege of meeting in groups. Christ is the Head and Lord of the church. Some churches may die because of extreme persecution, economic downturns, and other reasons. However, the church as God's people will continue until Jesus comes again. Soul-stirring music, personal testimonies, heartfelt praying, mission work, and solid Bible teaching blessed by the Holy Spirit will add life to the church. Let's consider a few references to the church from the following New Testament passages.

1. Matthew 16:13–20. Where were the apostles when Peter made His confession? What did Jesus tell Peter about the Rock of the church? What is the future of the church?

2. Acts 2:42–47. The church exploded in growth at Pentecost as the Holy Spirit filled the lives of believers. What kind of fellowship and relationships will change lives today?

3. Acts 8:1–4. Who led in the first persecution against the church? Where is opposition to the church happening today? What should persecuted believers do?

4. 1 Corinthians 3:11–17. Who is the foundation of the church? Why can't another foundation be laid? What or who constitutes God's holy temple?

5. Ephesians 1:22–23. What exclusive position must Christ have in His church? Where are all things in relation to Christ? Is Jesus always Lord of God's people today?

6. Ephesians 2:14–22. What did Christ do about the Jew and Gentile within the fellowship of believers? How does the church fellowship have access to God?

7. Ephesians 4:11–12. Who are a few of the leaders within the church? Why do they hold these positions? How do God's people build up the church and glorify God?

8. 1 Timothy 3:14–16. What instructions did Paul give the church? How did Paul identify the church (verse 15)? How is Jesus the secret of the church, or the mystery of godliness?

9. Philemon 1:2, 10–12. Philemon had a house church. Who was Onesimus (referred to in verse 10)? How can slaves and owners have fellowship? How can members help in restoring relationships?

10. 1 Peter 2:4–5. Why is Christ called the Living Stone (verse 4)? Who are the living stones and what spiritual sacrifices can we offer to God?

Comfort

When a baby cries at two in the morning, the child wants comfort. Either he is hungry or cold or needs some other attention from his parent. All of us call out in one way or another for comfort or encouragement at times. The word *comfort* means to make comfortable, relieve pain, or solve some problem. We live in a world full of hurts and pain and loneliness. Jesus set the perfect pattern for all of us to stand with others and give comfort and support when it is needed. The Bible speaks of comfort many times.

1. Genesis 24:67. Isaac was the son of Abraham and Sarah. When Sarah died, Isaac was sad and Rebekah comforted him. When have you needed comfort?

2. Job 2:11; 16:1–5. How did Job's three friends show him comfort? What happened later with Job and his friends? How did Job react? How can we show true comfort to someone who is grieving?

3. Psalm 94:19. When David felt anxiety-ridden, where did he find comfort? What did God's comfort do for David? How does God offer us help?

4. Isaiah 40:1–2. What commission did God give to Isaiah? How was he to speak to Israel? What was his message of comfort?

5. Isaiah 51:3. What good message did God have for Israel after their defeat and ruin? What would happen to their wastelands? Why can God's people sing again?

6. Matthew 2:16–18. Who was Rachel and what happened to her children? What were the circumstances of that tragedy? What is our hope in the face of sorrow?

7. John 14:1–16, 26–27. Why were the disciples saddened? What did Jesus promise to do for them? What does the Comforter do for believers?

8. Acts 9:26–31. How did the early Christians have the comfort of the Holy Spirit? What had they faced? How does the Holy Spirit strengthen and help us today?

9. Romans 15:1–4. How did the events of the past teach the followers of Jesus? How do we find comfort today in God's Word?

10. 2 Corinthians 1:3–7. Why did Paul write that God is the God of all comfort? When does God comfort us? How do our experiences prepare us to comfort others?

Commandments— the Ten

More than six hundred laws were added to the Old Testament commandments to satisfy the whims of religious leaders. We could probably never count the number of laws in any given country today that tell people how they should live.

God gave Moses the Ten Commandments around 1450 BC (Exodus 20; Deuteronomy 5). Jesus summarized those commands by saying that we should love God with our total being and love others as we love ourselves. If we practiced these two commands, most of our problems would be solved.

1. Exodus 20:1–3. The first command gives emphasis to the Giver of the Law. What did God do for His people? Why did God tell His people not to have other gods?

2. Exodus 20:4–6. What is an idol? Why didn't God want His people to worship idols? What happens to idol worshipers? What blessings do those who love God enjoy?

3. Exodus 20:7. How does a person take God's name in vain or misuse His name? Why is one guilty who curses or uses God's name in vain? When are we guilty of this?

4. Exodus 20:8–11. What does it mean to keep God's day holy? Who should rest one day each week? What does it mean that God rested after His act of creation?

5. Exodus 20:12. How does a person honor his or her mother and father? What promise is given to those who obey this command? How do you see this command violated today?

6. Exodus 20:13. Is there a difference between killing and murder? What about war? What about capital punishment? Discuss these issues.

7. Exodus 20:14. What is the definition of adultery (Matthew 5:28)? How did the Israelites disregard this command? What happens to family life when this command is ignored?

8. Exodus 20:15. Why is stealing so common? What are the various ways a person steals? Are we entitled to property rights?

9. Exodus 20:16. How does a person give false testimony against a neighbor? Where does this usually take place? How would you feel if someone told a lie about you?

10. Exodus 20:17. What does it mean to covet? Why do we sometimes want something that belongs to another person? Is coveting always wrong?

Confession

Sometimes when prisoners are taken captive during times of war, they may make true or false confessions because of punishment or other threats. Luke chapter 15 tells about a true confession of a prodigal who had wasted his possessions in sinful living. He said that he would go home and confess to his father about his sin. He did what he said he would do. His father welcomed him home and gave a huge celebration for him.

The word *confession* in Greek is *homolego*. That is, "I agree or confess by telling the truth." What would happen in the world if in our churches we had regular times of true confession? Here are a few references relating to confession.

1. Proverbs 28:13. What happens to a person who hides his sins? What happens if we confess and forsake our wrong? Why is God pleased when we confess our sins?

2. Daniel 9:3–9. Who did Daniel say had sinned and how did he confess those sins? When we confess our wrongs as Daniel did, what will God do?

3. Matthew 10:32. How do we acknowledge Jesus before others?

What happens to those who do not confess Jesus? What will Jesus do for those who identify themselves with Him?

4. John 12:42. Why did some leaders who believed in Jesus not make a confession of faith in Him? Why might it be difficult for some people to confess Christ before others?

5. Romans 10:9–10. What does it mean to confess Jesus as Lord? What happens to those who confess with their mouth and believe in their heart concerning Jesus?

6. Philippians 2:9–11. Does the world believe that the name of Jesus is above every name? What do you think about Christ's lordship? What does that confession mean to you?

7. 1 Timothy 6:12–14. What kind of confession did Timothy make? Who made a perfect confession before Pilate? How is Christ's confession a model for us?

8. James 5:16. What does it mean to confess our faults to one another? Is it easy to confess our faults and pray for someone against whom we have sinned?

9. 1 John 1:9. Why should our sins be confessed? To whom do we admit our sins? What happens when we confess sin? How does this verse apply to daily life?

10. 1 John 4:15. Do you believe that Jesus is the Son of God? Why does the Bible repeat this truth? What happens within a person who confesses that Jesus is God's Son?

Conflicts— Strife

Across the centuries conflicts have always occurred among the nations. From the outset of human history until the present day, politicians and prophets, military commanders and religious leaders, have searched for answers to the never-ending struggles we all endure.

In a bar or tavern, amid all the frolicking and laughter, a fight will erupt during Happy Hour. Conflicts sometimes run rampant within government circles and between political parties as well as in churches. Families know their share of strife. Troubles are universal. Life suffers if we fail to control our problems. The Bible gives us some examples of conflict and strife as well as some solutions.

1. Genesis 13:8–12. What problem did Abram and Lot's workers have? What solution did Abram offer? Is there a godly way to handle problems?

2. Proverbs 17:1. Would you prefer a simple meal with peace rather than a big banquet with a lot of contention? Why? How does this verse apply to family life?

3. Proverbs 18:19. What happens to a person who becomes offended

through a dispute? Is it easier to conquer a fortified city than a brother? Why is it so hard to appease an offended person?

4. Proverbs 20:3. Why is it an honor to avoid strife? Why do some Christians seem to cultivate the quarreling habit? Is God pleased with church wranglings? What does Scripture call a quarreling or meddling person?

5. Luke 22:20–26. A dispute broke out among the disciples about which one was the greatest. When did that happen? What did Jesus say? What do you say about it?

6. Acts 15:35–41. Why did Paul and Barnabas have a falling-out after their missionary trip? What did they do after they separated? What can we learn from their experience?

7. Romans 14:5–6. How do we resolve problems about what foods we eat and days of worship? Discuss Luke 10:8; Acts 11:6–9; 1 Corinthians 10:25, 31; and Titus 3:9.

8. 1 Corinthians 3:1–4. What problems did the church in Corinth have? How do God's saints reflect carnality instead of spirituality? What's the solution to these sins?

9. Philippians 2:3–4. Paul gave counsel to the Philippians about being unselfish and esteeming others better than themselves. How can we practice this attitude today?

10. James 3:13–18. What are some sources of disagreement? What are some of the damages of strife? How can peacemakers help? Do you cause disputes or help solve them?

Cross of Christ

18

Arthur Blessitt grew up in Mississippi. For nearly forty years he has carried a heavy cross on every continent. He has walked through all 315 countries in the world, sharing the message of Jesus face-to-face with thousands of people. He has also spoken about Jesus and the cross in churches and on television programs hundreds of times.

In ancient Rome, the government's principal way of execution was to crucify the condemned. Sometimes dozens of crosses stood on Roman roads, their victims hanging on those crosses to remind people not to rebel against Rome. Has the cross within believing communities lost its radical meaning? Do we see the cross as an ornament, or a life-changing experience? Look at some expressions of the cross as seen from the biblical perspective:

1. Matthew 16:24; Luke 9:23. What three requirements did Jesus give His disciples? Have we minimized these conditions for being Christ's followers?

2. Matthew 27:39–42. How did religious leaders ridicule Jesus as He was dying on the cross? Do you think the mockers would have believed in Jesus if He had come down from the cross?

3. John 19:19–22. What words were fastened to the cross where Jesus

was crucified? Why were those words written in Aramaic, Latin, and Greek? Why do you think Pilate wrote what he did?

4. 1 Corinthians 1:17–18. What did Christ call Paul to do? How can the cross become powerless? What does the cross mean to unbelievers? What does it mean to the saved?

5. Galatians 6:14. What was Paul's source for boasting? What did the cross mean to him? What does it mean to be crucified to the world?

6. Ephesians 2:16. How does being reconciled or brought back to God take place? What happens to the hostility that existed between man and God?

7. Philippians 3:18–19. Paul stated that many were enemies of the cross of Christ. What does that mean? How is hatred of the cross expressed?

8. Colossians 1:20. How are all things in heaven and on earth reconciled to God? What does the blood shed on the cross provide for the believer?

9. Colossians 2:13–15. What great transactions took place for the believer through the cross? What did Christ do with the Old Testament laws and ordinances that were against us?

10. Hebrews 12:2. What did Jesus expect beyond the cross? What cost was involved in Christ's death on the cross? Where is He dwelling now? To what or to whom should Christ's followers look for faith, inspiration, and hope?

Death—
Physical and Spiritual

We all know that physical death is a universal experience. Thousands of people die every day all over the world as a result of illness, accidents, wars, starvation, and many other causes. Death can occur at any stage of life—before birth, as a child, as a young person, in the middle years, or when we become old, or very old and feeble. Scripture gives us some insights about death.

1. Genesis 2:15–17. What did God tell Adam would happen to him if he ate of the forbidden tree? What *two* deaths did Adam suffer?

2. 2 Kings 20:1–7. What did Isaiah tell King Hezekiah? What is involved in "setting one's house in order"? Can we extend our life?

3. Psalm 23:4. Describe "the shadow of death." Who is with us always, even at the time of our death? What should be our reaction as we face death?

4. Psalm 116:15. How does God evaluate the home going of His people? Does the statement about death being "precious" have

more than one meaning? How should the Christian look at death?

5. Isaiah 57:1–2. What advantage does a believer have leaving this life? What is the state or condition of a departed saint? Why should death not be feared?

6. Romans 8:6, 13. What does it mean that a carnal mind leads to death? What kind of death? How can we truly live? What does it mean to die daily? (1 Corinthians 15:30–32).

7. 1 Corinthians 15:54–58. What question is asked of Death? What is the sting of death? What conquers death and removes the sting? Since Christ has gained the victory over death, how should we occupy ourselves in this life?

8. 2 Corinthians 5:1–5. What kind of body will God give believers when their earthly body dies? What guarantees a better life after death?

9. Philippians 1:21–24. What struggles do God's people often face before death? Would it be profitable for others if your death were delayed?

10. Revelation 1:18. How does Jesus' experience with death and resurrection give us a valid hope? Why does Jesus hold the keys to death and hell?

Depression or Despair

The apostle Paul had some experience with depression, but he always made a comeback. He wrote about being content in every situation, whether hungry or satisfied, with plenty or with nothing.

Jeremiah lived in a state of despair most of his life. King Jehoiakim cut Jeremiah's scroll into shreds and burned it (Jeremiah 36). However, God told Jeremiah to write it again (actually dictated to the scribe Baruch)—a long, hard job in 600 BC. Jeremiah suffered near-death prison time in a cistern with water up to his neck—an early version of water boarding? In Lamentations 3, he expressed his bitter feelings. Hope faded. But a new day dawned when Jeremiah discovered that God's mercies are new every morning. He wrote that man needs to wait for God's deliverance. With God's help, we too can get through tough times.

1. Genesis 27:46; 28:1–5. Why was Rebecca depressed about her son Jacob? Who helped her? How can we help people with difficult decisions avoid despair?

2. Numbers 11:10–17. Why did Moses feel depressed and blame God for his troubles? What did he ask God to do? What answer did God give Moses? How can we apply this story in our own lives?

3. Numbers 21:4–5. Why were God's people impatient and upset? Why did they blame God and criticize Moses for their predicament? Why were they in the desert in the first place? What daily routines today can be depressing?

4. Joshua 7:5–12. What did Joshua do in this stressful, daylong experience? What was his regret? What was God's answer?

5. 1 Kings 19:1–8. Why was Elijah in the desert? What did he want God to do to him? Have you ever felt like Elijah? How do bad experiences sometimes bring about good decisions?

6. Psalm 142:1–7. Who will listen to our complaints? What bad can happen when we are in the right place? What is our resource when no one seems to care about us?

7. Jonah 4:1–11. Why did Jonah say it would be better for him to die? Did he need a new focus? What would happen to our depression if we obeyed God?

8. Matthew 27:46. What did Jesus say as He was dying? Why did it feel like God had left Him? If Jesus could be depressed, this would certainly be the time.

9. Luke 15:20–21. What brought on the depressed state of the prodigal son? When a person's friends and money are gone, will depression be the natural outcome? What is the solution?

10. 2 Timothy 4:10, 16–17. Did Paul sound depressed in these verses? If your friends all forsook you, how would you feel? What help did Paul find? What is our hope in desperate times?

Discernment—
Understanding

21

The book of Genesis tells the story of Jacob's deception of his father, Isaac. Jacob and his mother concocted a plan so that Isaac would give his birthright blessing to Jacob rather than his older twin brother, Esau. When Jacob pretended to be Esau, telling Isaac that he had come for his blessing, Isaac felt Jacob's arms, which had been covered with goat's hair to resemble Esau's hairy arms. He said, "Your voice is the voice of Jacob, but you feel and smell like Esau." He was not able to discern the difference, and gave the blessing to Jacob. The Bible challenges us to discern the difference between the true and the false, the inferior and the superior.

1. 1 Kings 3:9. When Solomon became king, he asked God to give him a "discerning heart" to govern Israel. How does discernment help in families, work situations, church decisions?

2. Proverbs 7:6–27. When a man meets a prostitute who traps him, he is like an ox going to the slaughter. How would discernment help someone to recognize evil and allow good judgment?

3. Proverbs 10:4; 13:4. It takes more than desire to see success. It

must be accompanied by diligence. Why is the easy way, the obvious way, not always the right way?

4. Ecclesiastes 8:5. From the "wisdom book," a need is indicated for discernment about the right time and right procedure for every matter. How does this idea apply to our lives?

5. Ezekiel 44:23. Israel's priests taught how to know the difference between the secular and the sacred, the clean and unclean. Is this lesson lacking in today's churches?

6. Malachi 3:18. When God gathers His jewels, He will discern those who are righteous and those who are evil. How do we get ready for God's evaluation?

7. Luke 12:56. (See also Matthew 16:2–3.) Jesus told a few religious leaders that they could "discern the sky," but not the present time. What did Jesus mean by His words?

8. 1 Corinthians 2:14. Is a person able to discern the things of God without the Spirit of God? How can a believer know and use spiritual gifts? (1 Corinthians 12:7–10).

9. 1 Corinthians 11:26–30. What are some of the dangers of partaking of the Lord's Supper when one is not a believer or has not prepared himself to receive it? Do you think people generally do not take this sacrament seriously?

10. 2 Peter 3:10–14. Since the final day of the Lord will come like a thief in the night and end the world as we know it, how should we prepare ourselves and discern the signs of the times?

Dreams— Visions

22

Dr. Martin Luther King Jr. delivered one of the greatest speeches in history at the Lincoln Memorial in Washington, D.C., in 1963. One unforgettable quote from his discourse is: "I have a dream that one day, on the red hills of Georgia, the sons of former slaves and the sons of former slave owners will be able to sit together at the table of brotherhood." God's people need to seek God for His dreams and visions. Parents should plant and cultivate dreams and visions in the hearts and minds of their children. Church leaders need to inspire one another with visions about what God can do through His people to reach a hurting world. The Bible relates many stories of dreams that enlightened, instructed, challenged, and even caused people to tremble. Some of their lessons can be applied to our lives.

1. Genesis 15:1–5. What did God say to Abraham in a vision? What picture did God give Abraham of his descendants? Do you think God still speaks in visions and dreams?

2. Genesis 28:10–19. What did Jacob see in a vision? What did he determine he had seen that he called Bethel? What did God promise Jacob in verse 15?

3. Genesis 37:1–11. Describe Joseph's dreams. Has anyone ever opposed your dreams? How did Joseph's dreams relate to others? (Genesis 41:15–30).

4. Proverbs 29:18. What is the danger of no vision among God's people? How can vision change an individual's outlook or a church's responsibility to the nations?

5. Daniel 2:10–50. What did Daniel ask three friends to do about Nebuchadnezzar's dream? What did that king's dream reveal about the future? Who did Daniel credit with the dream's interpretation? Did the king acknowledge the source of the revelation?

6. Joel 2:28; Acts 2:17. What is the source of spiritual dreams and visions? Who has the dreams God gives? Have you experienced visions or dreams that you feel are from God?

7. Habakkuk 2:2–3. What action should be taken by those who have a vision from God? What is required of us who look for a vision from God?

8. Acts 11:5–18. Discuss the vision of Simon Peter. What was the interpretation of his vision? How could we apply this vision to our own lives?

9. Acts 16:7–10. What vision changed the direction of Paul's ministry? What kind of response did he make? Are there other visions that influenced God's work?

10. Jude 1:8. How did Jude, the brother of Jesus (Matthew 13:55; Mark 6:3), describe some dreamers? What are some outcomes of evil dreams?

Evangelism—
Witnessing

23

Larry Gross spent seventeen years in and out of jails in Pennsylvania. One day while out of prison, Larry read a gospel tract that someone had left on a park bench. Soon thereafter, the Lord saved the struggling, wayward great-grandson of a Jewish rabbi from Russia. Since that time, Larry has had an exciting romance with evangelism, telling people that they can know Jesus in a personal way and have a lifelong relationship with Him. Hundreds of people have stopped on highways and university campuses to talk with Larry about Jesus. He has spoken to thousands and has given out tens of thousands of gospel tracts. Some ask how they can witness for Christ. In any way the Holy Spirit leads, believers can be a testimony for Christ—by words, or by example. Several Scriptures challenge us to reach out to others with the Word of Life.

1. 2 Kings 7:3–9. Where were the four lepers and what was their ultimate decision? What did they do when they discovered that Israel's enemies had gone? How can we apply this story to our lives?

2. Psalm 126:5–6. Just as the farmer sows seeds and reaps a harvest, we can sow seeds as well. What is that seed? With what attitude

are we to sow the seed of the gospel? How will we return from such a venture?

3. Proverbs 11:30. Why is a person wise who wins others to Christ? What is the fruit of the righteous? In what ways is the one who witnesses blessed?

4. Isaiah 6:8, 11–12. What response did Isaiah have to the Lord's call to witness? How long did God tell Isaiah he should continue his work? Is the call to all God's people?

5. Daniel 12:3. What is the reward of a faithful witness? What metaphor is used for those who turn others to righteousness?

6. Matthew 28:18–20. By what authority do we witness to others? What should we teach? What are some of Christ's commands that are to be taught and practiced? How are we fulfilling the Great Commission?

7. Acts 1:8. How did the apostles become effective witnesses? Do we have access to the same power today? How can believers become involved in witnessing?

8. Acts 21:8–9. What do you think about Philip's four daughters and their ministry? What role can women have in ministry today? Describe some events in Philip's life (Acts 8:4–13; 26–40).

9. Acts 26:19–23. Who heard Paul's testimony? What was his message? What is our message? In what ways can we share the story of Jesus? How effective is our work?

10. 2 Timothy 1:1–10. How can a person who witnesses be strong? What should he or she teach others? What encourages a believer to proclaim God's Word (verse 10)?

Faith

24

Some of God's people across the centuries have had a weak faith and have doubted God. When Moses led the Israelites from Egypt across the Red Sea into the wilderness area south of the Holy Land, they complained to Moses. They said that in Egypt they had meat to eat, but they were going to starve to death where they were. Moses talked to God about the problem. God told Moses that He would give the people flesh to eat not just for one or two days, not for five, ten, or twenty days, but for an entire month. He said He would give them meat until it started coming out of their noses. Moses told the Lord that the Israelite men numbered 600,000 and that to feed them and their families meat for one month would require killing all their cattle and eating all the fish in the ocean. God said, "Just wait, Moses!" That night God sent a wind that brought so many birds into their camp that they could not begin to kill and eat them all (Numbers 11:22, 31; Exodus 16:13). What about our faith?

1. Deuteronomy 32:15–20. After God saved His people from Egyptian slavery, how did some show their unfaithfulness? What happens to those without faith?

2. 2 Chronicles 20:15–22. Why did God's prophet tell the king of

Israel not to be afraid when the enemy was ready to attack? What does such a faith-promise mean to us?

3. Matthew 17:20. What kind of faith moves mountains? How does God produce miracles? What "impossible" situation are you facing now?

4. Luke 17:5. What did the disciples ask Jesus to do for them? How does Christ increase our faith? In what areas of life do you need more faith?

5. John 6:28–29. The apostles asked Jesus what they must do in order to do God's works. What did Jesus say to them? What does it mean to believe on Jesus?

6. Ephesians 6:16. How important is a shield in battle? How does the shield of faith protect a person? Name a few fiery darts or flaming arrows we face.

7. Hebrews 11:1–3. Describe what faith is. How can we understand creation without faith? How does faith relate to creation?

8. Hebrews 11:6, 17–38. What does verse 6 say about faith in God? What is one specific way to please God? List the ways Old Testament people demonstrated their faith.

9. James 2:17. How does real faith express itself? If a person's so-called faith does not respond to the needs of others that can be at least partially met, what should we think about that kind of faith?

10. 1 John 5:4–5. How do you express your faith? How does faith lead believers to have victory over the world? What is the source of our faith? How is Jesus a present, every-moment reality in our lives?

Fasting

25

Almost everyone eats breakfast. After a night without food, some feel half-starved. The word *breakfast* means "break the fast." In Spanish, *desayuno* means *breakfast*. The Spanish word *des* carries the idea of stopping the *ayuno,* or fast. Thus in both Spanish and English we stop fasting when we begin to eat in the morning. Those who plan to fast should check with their doctors and have medical approval for any spiritual-physical journey of fasting. Even though we don't hear much about this habit except in the area of weight loss, we need to give attention to it. The following examples from the Bible should help us have a better understanding of fasting.

1. Deuteronomy 9:9, 18–21. Moses walked to the top of Mount Sinai and received the Ten Commandments. How long did he fast because of Israel's sins? Should we fast? What is the purpose of fasting?

2. 2 Samuel 12:15–23. David fasted while his first child was alive, although he was ill. When the baby died, he ended his fast and returned to his normal duties. Can you explain why he did this?

3. Ezra 8:21–23. When Ezra prepared to leave Babylon after the

captivity, what did he and the Hebrews do? What did they ask of God? What did God do for them?

4. Isaiah 58:1–14. The fast of some Hebrews ended in fighting. What kind of fast does God desire? What are the results of such a fast?

5. Jonah 3:5–10. About one hundred twenty thousand people in Nineveh heard Jonah preach for forty days. What did everyone do in response? What did God do? What can we learn from this story?

6. Matthew 6:16. Why was Jesus critical of the fasting habits of many religious leaders? How does God feel about those who openly display their religion? What does this teach us about rewards?

7. Luke 2:36–37. Anna was an eighty-four-year-old widow who was a prophetess. What had she been doing since her husband's death many years earlier? What message does this kind of dedication convey?

8. Luke 18:10–14. A Jew who collected taxes from his nation for the Roman government found acceptance with God. Why did the religious Pharisee not find the same acceptance?

9. Acts 13:1–3. The church in Antioch fasted and prayed. What message did the Holy Spirit give them? What happened next? What do you think about fasting?

10. Acts 14:21–23. Paul and Barnabas appointed leaders in several churches. In what two ways did they commit those leaders to the Lord? Is this a model for us?

Fellowship—Partnership

26

Aesop was a Greek writer who lived around 500 BC. In one of his fables, Aesop tells about a father with several sons who had problems among themselves. One day the father asked them to bring him some sticks. The man tied the sticks together and asked his sons to break the bundle of sticks, which they could not do. Then he gave each son a stick and told each one to break his stick. They did that very easily. Then he told the sons that if they stuck together, they would not be injured by their enemies, but if they were divided, their enemies could defeat them. Mark 3:14 states that Jesus called His apostles so that they would "be with Him." God's people become a partnership when we stick together in *koinonia* (Greek for "fellowship"). Fellowship with God comes about through a holy life. Christian fellowship involves ethical standards and practices. See what the following verses have to say about fellowship.

1. Psalm 133:1. What two words in this Scripture describe living together in unity? Name two or three areas where fellowship is pleasant or where it could be improved.

2. Acts 2:41–46. The church in Jerusalem "continued" in fellowship. How does verse 46 describe their unity? How can we become more like that early church?

3. 1 Corinthians 1:9–10. Who calls Christians into fellowship? What does this passage teach about good fellowship? How can churches or believers enrich their unity or togetherness?

4. 2 Corinthians 6:14–16. What kind of fellowship should we avoid? How did Jesus relate to "publicans and sinners" (Luke 7:34)? Describe the difference between friendship with sinners and being committed to them in marriage or business partnerships.

5. 2 Corinthians 8:1–6. What did the churches in Macedonia ask Paul to do? What is a fellowship ministry? How can we become involved in this kind of service?

6. Galatians 2:9. What does it mean that three apostles gave Paul and Barnabas the right hand of fellowship? How can we be partners in various ministries and outreaches?

7. Philippians 1:4–6. Why did Paul thank God for his relationship with the Philippians (4:17–19)? To what extent is God faithful to us?

8. Philippians 3:10–11. How did Paul experience the fellowship of Christ's sufferings? (2 Corinthians 11:25–26). Are we ready for that kind of partnership with Christ?

9. 1 John 1:3. What kind of relationship did John have with Christ? In what ways are our Father God and Christ His Son within our spiritual circle? How should this truth affect us?

10. 1 John 1:6–7. Are we having fellowship with Christ if we walk in darkness, or don't live as we should? What blessings are ours if we walk in spiritual light?

Fools

27

In centuries past, kings and other royalty sometimes had what were called court jesters. These entertainers often wore dunce caps and regaled their guests with outlandish words and activities. Often they were referred to as fools. A fool is a person who lacks wisdom and fritters his life away. Fools waste time thinking and doing the frivolous, with little thought toward important issues for themselves, their families, and others. The Bible refers to fools several times, cautioning people not to live in foolish ways. We will look at several verses from the Old and New Testaments that give insight into the life of a foolish or wasteful person.

1. Psalm 14:1; 53:1. Even with the evidence of creation, the Scriptures, Jesus, and history, the fool denies God's existence. How would you answer someone who denies that God is alive?

2. Psalm 107:17. How does a person become a fool? What are the consequences?

3. Proverbs 10:8, 10, 21, 23. Contrast the wise in heart and the chattering fool. What brings about a fool's death? Where does he find pleasure?

4. Proverbs 12:15–16; 13:16; 14:1. Is a fool confident of his own

way? What reactions are typical? What destructive ways make up a fool's life?

5. Proverbs 14:7–9. What actions describe a foolish man? What does he mock? Is there any hope for fools?

6. Proverbs 18:6–7; 24:7. What can a fool's words cost him? What kind of association does a fool miss? Why and where does a fool have nothing to say?

7. Ecclesiastes 10:12–15. How does a foolish person destroy himself? When does a foolish person stop talking? Why does work trouble a fool?

8. Jeremiah 4:22. How does Jeremiah describe the fool? Do you know anyone like this?

9. Luke 12:16–20. What are God's thoughts of a person who has no time or room for Him? What is the result? Why do you think people try to get along without God?

10. 1 Corinthians 4:10. What does it mean to be a "fool for Christ"? How can we imitate Paul's way of life? Are we ready to be a fool for Jesus if need be?

Forgiveness

28

Someone asked a young girl from an island in the Caribbean what she had learned since becoming a Christian. She answered, "I have learned to forgive the man who killed my father." Some of us may need to learn how to forgive ourselves. As we live day by day, we sometimes make wrong choices, doing what should not be done and not doing what should be done. We let our mistakes or sins hang around our neck like an albatross. As tough as the assignment may be, let's not hide behind excuses, but admit our wrong and forgive ourselves. Sometimes we get mad at God and blame Him because of our failures. When hurts are deep and bitterness seems justified, we may not want to forgive whatever or whoever has been involved in our lives. Forgiveness is not always easy; however, God's way is to forgive. Let's look at some Scriptures on forgiveness.

1. Exodus 10:16–17. When the plagues of locusts came upon Egypt, what did Pharaoh ask Moses to do? Did God forgive him? How does this story apply today?

2. Isaiah 55:6–7. Why should people seek the Lord? Who will God forgive or pardon if they will turn to Him? How is God's pardon described? Will God forgive us?

3. Jeremiah 31:34. Why should God forgive and forget our sins and never remember them anymore? How does He do that? Why should we forgive mistreatments?

4. Matthew 6:14–15. When we forgive someone who sins against us, what will God do? What if we refuse to pardon those who offend us? How can we afford not to forgive?

5. Matthew 18:21–22. Simon Peter asked Jesus if a person needed to forgive another more than seven times. What did Christ's answer mean? What is your response?

6. Luke 17:3–4. Do these verses surprise you? Has anyone ever upset you seven times in one day? What's the normal reaction to multiple offenses?

7. Luke 23:32–34. How did Jesus respond to those who mocked Him and crucified Him? Is Jesus our role model in forgiveness?

8. Acts 13:38–39. What message is preached through Jesus? What other ways do people seek forgiveness? Why can we not be justified through the Law of Moses?

9. Ephesians 1:7. What does it mean to be forgiven and redeemed through the blood of Jesus? How is God's grace described in this verse?

10. Colossians 3:13. How should we face or endure the grievances that come our way from others? How is God's forgiveness an example to follow? How should quarrels be resolved?

Friends

There is a town in Texas by the name of Friendswood. That growing city south of Houston began with a religious group called the Quakers, or Friends.

Several years ago, Dale Carnegie wrote a book entitled *How to Win Friends and Influence People*. That book helped change the lives of thousands of people across the globe.

A friendship circle with new and old friends is a blessing. The Bible reminds us of friendship links. Consider this fascinating topic of friends:

1. 1 Samuel 18:1–4. Who was Jonathan? When did his friendship with David begin and how long did it last? Friendship is a priceless gift—especially one as close as David and Jonathan enjoyed. Describe some of your friendships and what they have meant to you.

2. Job 2:11–13. Job's friends went to comfort him. Why is it sometimes best to sit quietly with a grieving friend rather than talk and ask questions? Later in the book of Job we see how his friends criticized him and even challenged his faith. What happens when we criticize friends?

3. Psalm 41:9. Who was the "false friend" of Jesus? (See Matthew 26:14, 47–50.) How do we betray Jesus?

4. Proverbs 17:17. State some ways that friendship expresses itself. Do friends always agree? Even with many friends we may succumb to ruin, but who sticks with us always? (Proverbs 18:24).

5. Zechariah 13:6. What were the wounds Jesus suffered in His body? Who of his friends wounded him as well? How do we wound Christ today?

6. Matthew 11:19. Did Jesus include some unusual people in His friendship circle? Should we be friends of non-Christians? Why or why not?

7. John 11:35–36. What did Jesus do when He stood near the grave of Lazarus that reminds us of His humanity? How can we encourage and support others at difficult times in their lives?

8. John 15:13–14. What did Jesus call His followers? How do Christ's friends prove their friendship? Do you have friends who need to become friends of Jesus?

9. James 2:23. Why was Abraham called "the friend of God"? What sacrifice was he ready to make for God? (Genesis 22:1–14). How do we show that we are God's friends?

10. 3 John 1:4. The greatest joy we can know is that our children walk with the Lord. Another joy is knowing our friends walk with Him. How can we help our friends find a relationship with God? List some joys of friendship.

Fruitful or Fruit

Grocery stores stock many kinds of fruit that come from countries all over the world. Name some unusual fruits. What's your favorite fruit?

The Bible mentions fruit and being fruitful many times. To be fruitful means to have an abundance, to have barns overflowing, to increase, to experience growth, and similar ideas. Let's look at God's idea of fruit and the fruitful life.

1. Genesis 1:11–12. God placed plants and trees on this earth. What is necessary for fruit trees to produce good fruit? What is necessary for Christians to be fruitful?

2. Exodus 1:7. The Hebrew people were in Egypt for 400 years. What words describe their fruitfulness during their slavery? What might be a reason for a people increasing in number?

3. Numbers 13:20–33. What report did the twelve spies give who spent forty days in Canaan? Why did most of Israel miss God's blessings in that fruitful land?

4. Psalm 92:12–15. The righteous are compared to a flourishing

palm tree. The promise is that God's people will produce good fruit even in old age. Does this encourage you to maintain a fruitful life to the end?

5. Matthew 7:15–23. False prophets are known by their fruit. What happens to those who do not produce good fruit? What is the message of verses 21–23?

6. Luke 13:6–7. A man cultivated fig trees for three years, but one tree had no fruit. What did the owner say to the worker? How does this parable apply to our spiritual lives?

7. John 15:1–2. What does God do with fruitless branches? How does God "prune" the good branches? What needs to be cut from our lives? How does this happen?

8. John 15:16. Why does Christ choose us? How do we know if our fruit is lasting? How does God bless those who are fruitful?

9. Galatians 5:22–23. Who makes possible the fruitful life? Discuss the fruit of the Spirit that this text speaks of. Do we produce the fruit? Where does it come from?

10. Colossians 1:10–12. What does it mean to "bear fruit in every good work"? What are some areas where we could be more fruitful?

Glorify—
Glorification

31

In 1798, Joseph Haydn (1732–1809) produced a musical work called *The Creation*. One year before his death, his friends took Haydn to hear the performance of that masterpiece in his home city of Vienna, Austria. As the orchestra and choir played and sang, they came to the words "And there was light." The crowd stood in applause. Haydn stood and, with trembling hands pointed heavenward, said, "No, no, not from me—from heaven above comes all!"

The words *glory, glorify,* and *glorification* appear more than five hundred times in the Bible. How blessed of God our nation and world would be if we would give glory and honor to the Lord in all things. Let's consider a few Scriptures that refer to God's glory and our challenge to glorify God, as well as the future glorification of believers and creation.

1. Exodus 33:18–23. What request did Moses make of God? Where did God place Moses before he saw the Lord's glory? Should we make that request today?

2. 1 Samuel 4:12–22. What tragic news did the Benjamite give to Eli? What happened when the wife of Phinehas heard that her

husband and father-in-law were dead? What did she name her son? Why does God's glory depart from a nation or church?

3. 1 Chronicles 29:10–13. Discuss the praise that David gave to God. What word did he use to describe God's name? Who is the source of wealth and honor?

4. Psalm 24:7–10. Who is the King of Glory? How does He fill our lives? How do we surrender, or yield our life to God?

5. Haggai 2:6–9. Who is the "Desire of all nations"? What promise did God give about the temple? Who makes up God's living temple? (1 Corinthians 3:16).

6. Luke 9:28–33. As Christ prayed, what happened to Him? Who appeared with Him in glorious splendor? What does this tell us of the afterlife?

7. Acts 12:21–23. What happened to Herod? Why? How can we glorify God in all that we do?

8. Romans 8:16–17, 21. As heirs of Christ, what will we one day share with Him? How will creation's decay be changed to glory? Do these events excite you?

9. 1 Corinthians 10:31–32. How can we glorify God in our daily habits of life? Why should we be concerned about not causing anyone to stumble in their faith? How can we guard against it?

10. 2 Corinthians 3:16–18. What removes the veil from a heart and life? Where is true freedom found? What glory awaits us and what should be our focus?

God

32

A story is told of a young boy who was drawing a picture. When someone asked what he was doing, he answered, "I am drawing a picture of God." When told that no one knows what God looks like, the boy responded, "They will when I get through with this!"

The Old Testament has several names for God, indicating different aspects of His being. The name *Elohim* appears 2,310 times and means "the majestic fullness of God." *Yahweh,* mistranslated *Jehovah,* appears about six thousand times in the Old Testament, such as when God said to Moses, "I Am that I Am," in Exodus 3:13. This refers to the fact that He is an eternal being. *Jireh, Rophe, Shalom,* and *M'Kaddesh* are other names connected with Yahweh. *Adonai* means "the Lord of Hosts." The names *El* and *Emmanuel* appear about two hundred times. *El–Shaddai* appears forty-five times. Look at these mind-expanding Scriptures about the person of God:

1. Genesis 1:1. *Elohim* (God) created the universe without any pre-existing material. Could an orderly universe have ever come about without a Designer? Why do you think some people deny this?

2. Exodus 15:11. God is unique. God is the Lord of Lords. Think about His attributes listed here. What other names are ascribed to God?

3. Exodus 34:5–7. Meditate on the seven awesome qualities of God listed here. How do these verses show that people are responsible before God?

4. 1 Chronicles 29:11–13. What qualities of God do these Scriptures emphasize? What is God's position before all things? What should be our response to God (verse 13)?

5. Isaiah 40:28–31. How is God described in these verses? Does the Creator ever become tired? What is His promise for those who become tired and weary? If you call on Him, you will know His strength.

6. John 17:1–3. How does God glorify His Son, Jesus Christ? What is the result of our knowing the only true God and Jesus Christ whom God has sent?

7. Acts 17:22–31. Notice how Paul picks up the inscription to an Unknown God and turns it into a declaration of who the true God is. Why are images of false gods so abominable? What is God's command to all men everywhere?

8. Romans 11:33–36. What do these verses tell us about God's wisdom, knowledge, and ways? Does God owe us anything? Can anyone teach or counsel God? (See Isaiah 55:8–9.) Discuss these ideas.

9. 1 Timothy 1:17; 6:13–16. What does it mean to describe God as the King eternal, invisible, and only God? Can there be any god higher than this God? What belongs to God forever?

10. 1 John 4:8–9. What one word best describes or identifies God? How did God demonstrate or prove His love to us? Do you know God in a personal way?

Gospel   33

Second Kings, chapter 7, tells the story of four Hebrew lepers who sat at the entrance of the city of Samaria. Syrian soldiers had camped around the city, and God's people within the city were dying from starvation. One of the lepers suggested that they go to the camp of the Syrians because it would not matter if the enemy killed them, since they were dying of starvation anyway. Considering their leprosy, they didn't have much to lose. When the four arrived near the camp of the Syrians, they discovered that their enemies had fled, leaving behind all their food and much more. The lepers devoured as much as they wanted, and then one said they needed to go tell their fellow Israelites what they had found. All of God's people soon began to celebrate because they had found food and the Syrian enemies had dispersed in fear.

We have the good news of the gospel to share with others. Many times we may be like the four lepers, delaying or hesitating to tell the story, but God's love constrains us to share it.

1. Isaiah 53:1–6. According to Isaiah, what is the message of the gospel? What does Christ do for those who believe? The gospel story from Isaiah is quoted in Acts 8:26–40, where Philip witnesses to the Ethiopian eunuch.

2. Matthew 4:23–25. Where did Jesus begin His ministry? What

is the gospel of the kingdom of heaven? What kind of work is involved in gospel proclamation?

3. Luke 2:8–11. Why did shepherds near Bethlehem become filled with fear? What did an angel say to them? Who is the world's only Savior and what is His mission?

4. Romans 1:16. How did Paul show that he was not ashamed of the gospel? What is the gospel? Who is included or excluded in the good news of Jesus?

5. 1 Corinthians 9:14. God ordains that those who preach the gospel should live by support from the church. What if a church cannot support full-time workers?

6. 1 Corinthians 15:1–5. What does the gospel do for the believer? What three basic truths compose the gospel? Name a few who first saw the resurrected Christ.

7. Galatians 1:6–8. Even today people sometimes leave the gospel they have been taught and seek another "gospel." How is truth sometimes diluted? Why do some add to or change God's Word? What does God say about those who preach another gospel?

8. Ephesians 6:19–20. The mystery of the gospel is that God wants to save everyone. How did Paul share the gospel? Did Paul have more reason to fear sharing the good news than we do today?

9. Philippians 1:12. What is Paul referring to that caused the furtherance of the gospel? How can bad experiences sometimes be used to advance the gospel?

10. Revelation 14:6. What did the angel in this vision carry? Why is the gospel referred to as eternal? Where is the gospel to be preached? What are we doing to make this happen?

Government or Civic Life

34

Evangelist Dwight L. Moody once took a strong stand about a political issue in Chicago. Someone rebuked Moody by reminding him that he was a "citizen of heaven." Moody responded, "Yes, that's true, but at the present time I vote in Cook County, Illinois."

Whatever a person's religious persuasion may be, he or she has a responsibility to God and the government. A biblical examination of the believer's relationship to the government or civic responsibilities may be encouraging to some and a puzzle to others. What response should we make when elected officials fail to follow godly principles or do not work for the well-being of the citizens of their city or country? Let's study what the Bible says about our duties to the government.

1. Psalm 2:2–6. Why and how do some governments try to break away from God? What is God's response? What happens to those who oppose God?

2. Daniel 2:19–24. Who has the final control of world empires? How does God set up and remove leaders? What will finally happen to world kingdoms?

3. Matthew 10:16–20. How did Christ warn His followers? If

Christians are tried because of their faith, how should they respond? How does the Holy Spirit help?

4. Matthew 22:15–21. Who asked Jesus about paying taxes? What did Jesus ask His critics to show Him? What did Jesus say about paying taxes to the government?

5. Luke 2:1–4. Why did Joseph and Mary make a ninety-mile trip to Bethlehem? Was their journey an easy one? Should they have protested about paying taxes to Rome?

6. Romans 13:1–3. Who ordains governments? Why should we be subject to and respect leaders? When it comes down to obeying God or rulers, whom should we obey? (Acts 5:29). Talk about some situations.

7. Romans 13:4–7. What can rulers do to those who are evil? Why pay taxes to the government? What three things do we owe our government according to verse 7? What would happen if we had no government? (Judges 21:24–25).

8. 1 Peter 2:13–17. What are some reasons for obeying civic rulers? What should be our attitude toward authorities? Sometimes doing God's will requires extreme measures (2 Corinthians 11:32–33).

9. 1 Timothy 2:1–4. Are we expected to pray for government leaders? What pleases God, and what does He want us to do to bring this about?

10. Revelation 11:15–17. Who is included in the world's kingdoms? When will the kingdom of this world become the kingdom of our Lord and of His Christ? The government will be on Christ's shoulders and it will have no end (Isaiah 9:6–7).

Grace

35

Early on the morning of December 8, 2005, my son who lives in San Antonio, Texas, called me. He knew something was wrong because he could only hear "mumbo-jumbo." On the way to my home in Laredo, he called the sheriff's department and a hospital, and a deputy sheriff and an ambulance were dispatched to my small town east of the twin cities on the Rio Grande. The ambulance driver and attendants found me and rushed me to a hospital in Laredo. A neurosurgeon "happened" to be in the emergency room, did a brain scan, drilled a hole to relieve the pressure on the brain, and removed a blood clot. A day later I said to the doctor in ICU, "Doctor Estrada, you saved my life." The doctor pointed toward heaven and said, "God did it." Grace means God's "favor," His love and kindness that we don't deserve. Let's talk about God's grace.

1. Genesis 6:8. In the ancient world when men became evil, Noah alone found favor in God's eyes. By God's grace, Noah was blameless. How does God's grace help us all to live as well as prepare us for eternity?

2. Luke 2:36–40. At twelve years of age, Jesus was filled with wisdom and grace. What is the occasion of this text? What does it mean to say that Jesus grew in grace?

3. John 1:14, 17. What does "the Word became flesh" mean? Where was Jesus before He came to the earth? What does it mean that He was full of grace and truth?

4. Acts 4:33. Much grace was upon the apostles. If we keep giving witness to Christ's resurrection, in what ways will God's grace also be upon us?

5. Romans 6:1–5. How bountiful is God's grace? Can we exhaust it? Should we sin more in order to receive more grace? What does Paul say about that? How do we unite with Christ in all that He accomplished for us?

6. Romans 11:5–16. Paul refers to a remnant saved by grace. Who are they? If salvation came through rites and sacraments, or so-called "good works," what purpose would grace have?

7. 2 Corinthians 12:9. When tough times come, what is our hope? Why can we joyfully face trials and tribulations? What is the result of God's grace? What is perfected in our weakness?

8. Hebrews 4:16. What does the throne of grace mean? How should we approach God's throne? What is the result of going to God with confidence?

9. James 4:6. Since God promises more grace, what kind of a person receives that grace, or unmerited favor? Who does God oppose?

10. 2 Peter 3:16–18. To avoid error, and falling from our position in Christ, how can we grow in God's grace? Think about these verses in terms of your own spiritual growth.

Health—
Healing

36

Hospitals and health clinics are as numerous across the world as cactus and mesquite are in South Texas. People want to have good health, even though many fail to live in a way that gives them an opportunity to enjoy the benefits that come through healthy bodies and minds. We spend billions of dollars on prescription drugs, vitamins, and exercise machines every year as we try to recover our health or enhance our total well-being. What about our national obesity problem? (Proverbs 23:1–3). The Bible speaks clearly about the health of saint and sinner alike. A study of a few Scriptures may help us see that God takes an interest in our health and healing.

1. Exodus 15:22–26. When the Israelites left Egypt, they found bitter water. How did it become sweet? How can bitterness of spirit affect one's health? What is the reward for listening carefully to the voice of the Lord and obeying His commands?

2. 2 Kings 2:18–21. What did Elisha do to change the bad water in Jericho? Can you name a few changes in your life habits that would improve your health?

3. 2 Chronicles 7:14. What steps must be taken for national

healing to occur? How does God help His people who follow His prescription?

4. Proverbs 3:5–8. What can bring health and nourishment to one's body? Do verses 5 and 6 hold potential for better health? Is it worth it to give up our own way to follow God's way?

5. Isaiah 58:6–8. How is taking our eyes off ourselves and looking to the needs of others a prescription for health? God's concern for the poor is great, and ours should be too.

6. Jeremiah 3:20–23. One spiritual illness is called backsliding. What does this mean? What social situation is compared to this? What is required to find relief from this malady?

7. Matthew 4:23. Part of God's message of salvation includes healing. After teaching in the synagogues, Christ was able to heal the sick. What kinds of illness did He heal, according to this verse? Talk about why healing isn't always a part of the Christian message in today's churches.

8. 1 Corinthians 12:7–10, 28, 30. The power to pray for healing is a gift of the Holy Spirit. Who actually does the healing in answer to prayer? Does everyone have the gift of healing? What are some other gifts of the Holy Spirit?

9. James 5:10–16. Whose example of patience and effective praying does James use? Do you think praying for recovery always has a positive outcome? Why or why not?

10. 3 John 1:2–4. Why do you think John prayed that his friend would enjoy good health for his body as well as his soul? What brought the greatest joy to John? What is even more important than physical health?

Heaven

37

A legend is told about a Christian who died. Upon arriving in heaven, an angel escorted him around the city. He was tremendously impressed as he passed up and down the streets of gold. He gazed upon mansion after mansion, wondering when the angel would show him his palace. Finally they came to the outskirts of a town and the angel stopped in front of a small cabin. As they started up the steps of the humble place, the Christian asked, "Why are we stopping here?" The angel told him this was his place. The Christian wanted to know why he didn't have a palatial home like the others they'd seen. The angel told him engineers had built his house out of the stuff he'd sent up before he arrived.

What is heaven going to be like? Our eternal inheritance comes from God's grace through faith in Jesus Christ and our commitment and service to the Lord while we travel the pilgrim's pathway.

1. 2 Kings 2:9–12. What did Elisha ask of Elijah as they walked along? Why do you think Elijah was swept away in a fiery chariot to heaven? What reward awaited him?

2. Matthew 6:19–21. What can happen to our earthly goods? What kinds of treasures can we lay up in heaven? Where is our heart when we send investments on ahead?

3. Luke 10:10–20. Christ's disciples had been on a mission. What exciting stories did they tell when they returned? For what better reason did Jesus tell them to rejoice?

4. John 14:1–4. What did Jesus indicate awaits His people in heaven? Who is preparing for your arrival in heaven? What does Jesus promise His followers in verse 3?

5. Acts 1:7–11. What mission is ours while we wait for Jesus to return? What did the two men in white tell the apostles after Jesus was taken up?

6. Acts 7:51–56. Stephen's words obviously incensed his hearers. What was the result of his being so outspoken? What did he see just before he died? What picture do you have of heaven?

7. 2 Corinthians 5:1–3. What happens when our earthly bodies wear out? What can we expect to have in heaven if we have received Christ as our Savior? What does Paul mean by his statement in verse 3?

8. 2 Corinthians 12:1–6. Who was Paul writing about in this text? What happened to him in the vision? Where is the "third heaven"? How did he describe his experience?

9. Hebrews 12:18–25. Describe Moses' vision of heaven. What has Jesus done for all believers (verse 24)? What is the warning of verse 25?

10. Revelation 21:1–4; 22:1–5, 15. (See also Isaiah 65:17.) Where does the new heaven and new earth come from? What does it mean that the old order of things will pass away? Describe the river of life. Is there room in heaven for the sexually immoral, murderers, and idolaters?

Hell

38

Hell is a word that incites fear and disdain, even denial on the part of some. What does it mean? Did Jesus teach about hell? What did He say about it? A number of years ago, the late Dr. John Newport of Southwestern Baptist Seminary was teaching on the topic of "Last Things" in a church in Houston, Texas. At the end of one of the sessions, a man said to him, "Dr. Newport, I didn't realize people still believed in hell." The highly esteemed professor, who had taught in several seminaries and universities, answered, "As far as I know, the doctrine is still in the Bible." Let's look at a few Scriptures that give some insight into the place where the unrighteous go at the end of this life, or after the final day of judgment.

1. Matthew 5:21–22. Though it isn't hard to believe murderers are in danger, what about people who remain angry with their brother or who call another a "fool"? What are your thoughts about hell?

2. Matthew 10:28. Why should we not be afraid of death? What is the greater thing to fear? Who has the power to destroy both body and soul in hell?

3. Matthew 18:7–9. How serious is it to cause others to sin? What

drastic action is described here to convey the offense of sinning with our bodies? Does this Scripture literally mean we should pluck out an offending eye? Discuss the possibilities.

4. Matthew 23:28–33. What strong words of condemnation did Jesus use against the New Testament religious leaders? What question did they face in verse 33? What does this tell us about appearances?

5. Matthew 25:41, 46. Who are we serving when we serve the poor and others who need our help or comfort? When Christ returns, what will He say to those on His left? What punishment awaits the unredeemed? What reward awaits the righteous (in Christ)?

6. Luke 16:19–31. Where was Lazarus taken each day to beg for food? What happened to him after he died? What happened to the rich man at whose gate he waited? What requests did the rich man make from hell? What was he told? Is there ever a second chance to make amends after death?

7. 2 Thessalonians 1:8–10. When Jesus comes again, what will He say to those who have rejected Him? What does "everlasting destruction" mean?

8. James 3:6. What damage can the tongue cause? How is the tongue like a fire? Discuss how the tongue can be controlled.

9. 2 Peter 2:1–10. What is the danger of false religious teachers? What will happen to them? How did God treat angels that sinned? What about the unrighteous? Who will be rescued from trials?

10. Revelation 20:14–15. What is thrown into the lake of fire? What happens to those whose names are not written in the Book of Life? How can a person avoid the second death?

Help 39

Dr. Hoke Smith served as a missionary in Colombia and Argentina. One day his four-year-old son came to him with a big apple, saying, "Daddy, help me get this apple started." We are like children who many times a day say, "Help me."

Every place we go we see people who need help, whether it's with financial problems, school challenges, home life, health issues, or conflicts in national and international relations. The story in every town, city, and nation is that people long for help. As believers in Jesus Christ, we need to follow Christ's example and the example of millions across the centuries who shared the Good Samaritan attitude and action and extended a helping hand to those in need. The Bible speaks in clear language about the topic of helping. Look at the following Scriptures:

1. Genesis 2:18. After the Lord made Adam, He made Eve to be his helper. A wife and husband help each other. Discuss how family members help one another.

2. 1 Samuel 7:12. What was the name of the stone that Samuel placed near Mizpeh? What is the definition of *Ebenezer*? How has God helped you through recent struggles?

3. 2 Samuel 9:1–7. Who was Mephibosheth? How did David help

him? How can we help those who need it? Who can you help today?

4. Job 6:11–13. Job faced many losses. What were they? He didn't have the strength to keep going. What happened to his resources? Who do you turn to for help in troubled times?

5. Isaiah 41:10. Why don't we have to be fearful? How does God help us when our lives are filled with problems?

6. Acts 16:9. Paul, Silas, Luke, and Timothy were missionaries. Why did their plans change direction? How can we help in the work of missions?

7. Romans 15:1–6. In what ways can strong believers help those who are weak? What attitude should we have toward the weak in our midst? What are the benefits of unity?

8. 1 Corinthians 12:28. We all have gifts. How would you describe a person with the gift of helps, or "able to help others"?

9. 2 Corinthians 1:10–11. Paul asked others to pray for him in time of great need. In what ways did their prayers help? What response did Paul anticipate from others when their prayers were answered?

10. Philippians 4:3. Among Paul's helpers, he named several women (Romans 16:1–16). How did they help Paul? How were they helped? Make a list of those you can help and those you can count on for help.

Holy Spirit 40

The late Dr. A. J. Gordon, eminent Bible teacher, told of an Englishman visiting an American friend. The American said to him, "Come. Let me show you the greatest unused power in the world." When they looked at Niagara Falls, the man from England said, "No, the greatest unused power in the world is the Holy Spirit."

The Holy Spirit is the Spirit of power. He glorifies Jesus Christ and is our guide to doing God's will and glorifying Him. We need to let the Spirit of God fill us and use us for His purposes. Let's review a few truths about the Holy Spirit found in the Bible.

1. Genesis 1:2. God's Spirit hovered over chaos and brought order into being at the time of creation. What does this say about the Holy Spirit? What can He do for you and me?

2. Genesis 6:1–6. How were people living in Noah's day? Why did God say His Spirit would not always strive or contend with man? Why is it dangerous to resist the Holy Spirit?

3. Matthew 12:31–32. Is the Holy Spirit a person? What is the sin against the Holy Spirit? Why can't that sin be forgiven? How can people commit that sin today?

4. Luke 4:16–19. What did Christ's anointing by the Spirit prepare Him to do? What is the meaning of spiritual anointing? How does the Spirit anoint a believer?

5. John 14:26. Who sent the Holy Spirit to live within God's people? When did that happen? What is the ministry of the Holy Spirit within us now? (Romans 8:26).

6. John 16:8–14. What is the Holy Spirit doing in the world today? How does the Holy Spirit bring about conversion? How does the Holy Spirit glorify Jesus?

7. Acts 1:4–8. Why did Jesus tell the apostles to stay in Jerusalem? What happened to them when the Holy Spirit came? How does He equip us to witness?

8. Acts 2:1–12. When Jesus returned to heaven, He sent the Holy Spirit, who lives in God's people. Discuss the events of Pentecost and how the Holy Spirit came upon the worshipers.

9. Acts 8:26–34. An angel of the Lord gave specific directions to Philip as to where he should go. As he obeyed, he met an Ethiopian official. How did the Holy Spirit direct Philip regarding the man? Do you think the Holy Spirit leads people to places of service today?

10. 1 Corinthians 12:3–12. (See also Romans 12:6–8; 1 Peter 4:10–11.) Discuss some gifts of the Spirit. Why does God give spiritual gifts? Do you know what your gifts are? Do these lists include all the spiritual gifts? Are there others you could name?

Hope

When voters elected Bill Clinton as president of the United States in 1992, countless people heard more about his hometown of Hope, Arkansas. However, *hope* is more than a town, a noun, or a person's name. Biblically, the word refers to something that is anticipated with the assurance that it will become a reality. For example, two disciples were talking as they walked to Emmaus from Jerusalem on the day of Christ's resurrection. The Savior appeared in their midst and asked why they were so sad. The two did not recognize Jesus and began to tell Him that the Messiah had been crucified and that they had hoped He would redeem Israel. Their joy overflowed as they discovered that the Savior was alive and present with them. Biblical hope has countless blessings. The Bible refers to hope about one hundred fifty times. Let's explore this life-changing theme.

1. Psalm 16:8–11. (See also Acts 2:26.) What does the psalmist mean when he says he rests in hope? Name some blessings that come because of the hope of the resurrection.

2. Jeremiah 17:7–8. Why should a person place his hope in the Lord? How does a tree by the side of a river stay alive during dry seasons? How is hope like a river?

3. Romans 5:1–2, 5. (See also 8:24–25; 15:13.) What is God's glory? What is our future hope? What does God fill us with as we trust in Him?

4. 1 Corinthians 15:17–19. The Christian's hope is in the resurrection of Christ. If this were not true, what would happen to our faith?

5. Ephesians 1:18–21. After Paul's conversion, his spiritual eyes were opened. Discuss the hope of our calling as it is related to salvation, service, sanctification, and glorification.

6. Colossians 1:5, 27. What is the hope stored for us in heaven? What does "Christ in you" mean to you? How can this truth enrich your life?

7. Titus 1:1–2; 2:13. On what basis do we hope for eternal life? What sort of lives should we live, awaiting this blessed hope prepared for us?

8. Hebrews 6:18–19. (See also 7:19.) What are we to do because of the hope that God puts before us? Describe the hope that is an "anchor for the soul." Why can't the Law of old give hope?

9. 1 Peter 1:3. (See also 3:15–16.) Why do Bible believers have a living hope? What does this kind of hope guarantee? What preparation does the passage 3:15–16 speak of?

10. 1 John 3:1–6. What change will take place in us when Christ returns? What happens to everyone who carries this hope in his heart?

Humility 42

John Newton, a converted slave trader in the 1700s, wrote the hymn "Amazing Grace." When he was near death, a young pastor came to visit him, lamenting the fact that England was losing a great hymn writer and preacher. Newton told the friend that he knew his life was coming to an end. Then he said, "If you look for me in heaven, you may find me at the feet of the thief on the cross who died believing in Jesus." After he was converted, the spirit of humility engulfed the life of John Newton. Perhaps we need to place ourselves on that route. Let's look at a few references on the theme of humility.

1. Genesis 18:1–10. Abraham greeted three visitors not knowing who they were. He had water brought so they could wash their feet and rest. Then he asked his wife and a servant to prepare a meal. Are we ready to greet strangers and make them comfortable? Who were these men and what was their message to Abraham?

2. Proverbs 16:18–19. What attitude does a person often have before he runs into a lot of trouble? What is better than sharing life with the proud?

3. Isaiah 57:15. How is God described in this verse? Who can have

fellowship with God? What benefits come to those who are contrite and humble?

4. Micah 6:6–8. What does the person coming before the Lord in worship list as possible ways to come into His presence? Name the Lord's only three requirements in verse 8.

5. Matthew 18:3. What does God ask us to become in order to enter the kingdom of God? Why do you think this is the only acceptable attitude?

6. Luke 14:7–11. What should be our choice of seats as an invited guest? Why is it more honorable to be exalted than to exalt oneself?

7. John 13:12–17. What did the disciples fail to do at the Last Supper? Why do you think they acted as they did? What did Jesus do for them? What example did He set for them?

8. Acts 20:17–20. How did Paul serve the Lord? What trials did he face? How do you think you would act under the circumstances Paul constantly faced?

9. Philippians 2:5–8. Describe how even Christ's birth showed His humility. What was His relationship to God? What was the crowning act of Christ's humility?

10. 1 Peter 5:5–6. What does it mean to be clothed with humility? What special gift does God give to the humble? Whom does God exalt? Have you ever experienced this?

Hunger or Hungry

43

Quite often we see people on a busy thoroughfare or in a poor area of town with a sign that reads something like this: *Help: Homeless and Hungry*. Official estimates state that at least one billion people in the world barely survive—consuming fewer than 1,800 calories a day.

What is the cause of such unfortunate conditions? Answers vary. Economic downturns have ruined a lot of people. Many jobs are shipped out of the country, leaving some without work. Others have a lifestyle that leads to poverty. Some squander what they have and bite the hand that feeds them. Some would blame it on bad luck.

About one half of the world's population goes to bed hungry every night. Some of these people sleep under bridges, in abandoned buildings, and in other places that at least provide shelter from the heat, cold, and other dangers. How can God's people help the hungry and suffering?

1. Deuteronomy 15:7–8, 11. How can we open our hands to the poor? Should we always show generosity toward the poor? What about poverty-stricken nations?

2. Job 22:1–8. What false charges did Eliphaz bring against Job? Why did Eliphaz make those accusations? Do we always know who is helping the destitute? Can we know another's motives?

3. Proverbs 19:15. Do problems come to some in society because they refuse to work? What happens to a lazy man? Should we help those who won't work?

4. Isaiah 58:9–11. How can we spend ourselves on behalf of the hungry? Why should we help those in need? How will God bless those who help the hurting?

5. Jeremiah 38:9–13. Who reported Jeremiah's condition to Judah's king? What kind of person do you think Ebed-Melech was? Many situations simply require that someone act. How can we help those who are mistreated?

6. Luke 4:1–2. How did Jesus suffer as He began His ministry? Discuss how temptation is greater when we are in a vulnerable position. Are God's people exempt from temptation or hardship today?

7. Luke 6:24–28. Who do these verses speak to? What good is abundance if it is not shared with the poor? How are we to answer those who mistreat us?

8. Luke 15:3–7. What value does God place on one who is lost? Should we be willing to help those who wander off? When safe in the fold, it is easy to lose sight of those outside. Discuss this reality.

9. 1 Corinthians 4:8–13. How did Paul describe the difficulties of the apostles? Positions of leadership and service are not always as they seem. Do you know of some in these positions who suffer today?

10. Revelation 7:14–17. What does this passage describe? Do you think the anticipation of this reward and comfort sustains those in hard places of service? Is serving God worth any sacrifice? Share stories you know of those who have suffered for Christ.

Husbands— Marriage

44

One definition of a husband is "one who plows." He takes care of his farm. Another definition of a husband is "a man who cares for his wife and family." This means that he provides diligent care for his family just as a farmer plans and works to have the best year possible on his farm. The husband's place is the spiritual head of the family, one who shows concern for the total well-being of each member of his household. Governments may make laws about marriage that run counter to the Bible, but everyone reaps the bitter fruit of any distortion of God's plan for marriage. God's only design for marriage is between a man and woman, and until recently this has been the only legal definition of marriage. God loves every individual, but does not approve of sin, no matter what kind of sin it may be. As Christians, we should love everyone but not condone a corrupt lifestyle. A doctor who gives a correct diagnosis of a patient's illness is not guilty of hating the patient for telling him the truth. Let's look at God's prescription for the family.

1. Genesis 2:18, 21–24. God said it is not good for man to be alone. How did He resolve this at creation? What is God's design for marriage?

2. 1 Samuel 1:6–8, 11, 20. Why was Elkanah disturbed? How did

he try to comfort his wife? What did God do for their joy? How can husbands comfort their wives?

3. 2 Kings 4:8–10. What did the woman of Shunem suggest to her husband? Is it a good idea for husbands to listen to the suggestions of their wives? Why or why not?

4. Proverbs 31:11, 23. How does the conduct of a wife affect the reputation of a husband? Why should husbands trust their wives? What blessings come to a couple who share a harmonious relationship?

5. Isaiah 54:5–7. Who is our true husband, whose care for us is unmatched? How does God show His concern for us? How does God's care for you give you encouragement?

6. Matthew 19:3–9. God's ideal for a husband and wife is that they never divorce. However, breakups sometimes happen. Although there are no simple answers for marital problems, what can you share from your own experience?

7. 1 Corinthians 7:2–4. Why does God say that the husband and wife will become one? Why is it important that they love and remain true to one another?

8. Ephesians 5:22–25. How does Paul describe the love a husband should have for his wife? Is this an easy command? How would this kind of love solve most unhealthy relationships?

9. Colossians 3:19. Paul adds another admonition to the command to husbands to love their wives. How can harshness be avoided? Does a husband's treatment of his wife affect other relationships in the home?

10. 1 Peter 3:7. Why should the husband be considerate of his wife? How is this shown? What gift do they share? How does this consideration affect their prayer life?

Hypocrisy 45

There are hypocrites all over the planet. A hypocrite is a person who doesn't really believe what they say they believe. They aren't who they appear to be. The word *hypocrite* means "false face." The origin of the word had its roots in the Greek and Roman plays. During the plays, the actors would often wear masks. When the show was over, the masks came off and they were back to their normal lives. Most ladies put on makeup before going out in public, and men have their own methods of looking good for others. Of course, there is nothing wrong with improving one's physical appearance. But we are all guilty of hypocrisy. Jesus called many religious leaders hypocrites. Let's look at what Scripture has to say about hypocrisy.

1. Isaiah 29:13. Is it possible to honor God with our mouth and not with our heart? Jesus quoted Isaiah in Matthew 15:7–9. Do we still have religious hypocrites in our churches today? Give examples of how this can be recognized.

2. Ezekiel 33:30–32. God told Ezekiel that people were saying negative things about him. When they heard him speak, what was their reaction? How is this information similar to what we see or hear today in our churches or neighborhoods?

3. Matthew 6:1–4. Should we always give to the needy? What do these verses teach about our attitude and actions when we give? How can giving be hypocritical?

4. Matthew 6:5. Where is a good place to pray? Why is private prayer better kept private? How should we not pray?

5. Matthew 6:16–18. What is the reward for fasting so others can see what we are doing? What is the purpose of fasting? What is our reward for fasting for the right reasons and without advertising what we are doing?

6. Matthew 23:27–32. What are the Pharisees called in this passage? Can righteousness be in appearance only? What is true righteousness and where does it come from?

7. Mark 12:10–17. What were some religious leaders trying to do to Jesus? How did they test Him? What did Jesus tell them to do?

8. Luke 6:41–42. Is it easy to see faults in another person's life and overlook what is wrong in one's own life? What did Jesus say we should do about it? Tell how this can be done.

9. 1 Timothy 4:1–5. What did Paul say many professing believers would do in the last days? Why is it wrong to forbid marriage or certain foods? What sanctifies these things for us?

10. 1 Peter 2:1. What are we to rid ourselves of? Is hypocrisy one of them? How can we learn to avoid this tendency?

Inheritance 46

Many people through the centuries have inherited fortunes; some squander what they receive while others use their inheritance for the glory of God and the good of others. But what about a spiritual inheritance that lasts forever? Do we have a vital interest in what God can give us that has everlasting value? Let's take a look at some Scriptures that give insight into God's promises about things that never come to an end.

1. Exodus 34:8–9. Moses prayed for God to forgive Israel's sins and take them as His heritage, or inheritance. What does it mean when God takes us as His heritage? Does He get a good bargain?

2. Job 27:13–15. Job felt overwhelmed at the success of evil people. But what do these people receive as an "inheritance"?

3. Psalm 16:5–7. Who is the believer's everlasting heritage? What does it mean that we have a delightful inheritance? What are some added benefits?

4. Psalm 119:111. David wrote that God's Word became his inheritance forever. Name some ways the Word gives us joy. How do we inherit the Bible?

5. Psalm 127:3–4. What are the blessings of having children? The

psalmist says they are our reward. In a good relationship between parents and children, these blessings and rewards extend into old age. Share how this has been true for you or others you know.

6. Matthew 25:34–36. If we serve others as unto God, what inheritance will we receive? Who is preparing our inheritance? Talk about how easy it is to see only the person we serve and not the Lord.

7. Luke 15:12. The prodigal son demanded the inheritance due him before the proper time. How is timing important in these issues? What can parents teach children about waiting and about valuing their heritage?

8. Ephesians 5:5. What bars someone from receiving an inheritance from God? How can someone receive God's inheritance? (Revelation 22:14).

9. Hebrews 11:8. How did Abraham receive his inheritance? How is he the father of all who believe? What inheritance awaits us?

10. 1 Peter 1:3–5. How long does an inheritance generally last? What about God's inheritance for His people? Where is it kept?

Jesus Christ—His Humanity

47

More than six billion people live on the earth today. We are all part of the human family. For centuries questions have been debated about the humanity and the deity of Jesus. Is Christ both human *and* divine? The Bible calls Jesus "Son of Man" as well as "Son of God." He is fully God and fully man. The apostles lived with Jesus for three years and knew Him as the majestic Christ and sinless man. Peter wrote in his first epistle (2:22) that He was without guile or sin. Jesus is the only person who has lived a perfect life. He was born without sin, lived without sin, and yet in His physical death "became sin for us." He is the amazing Christ. Eternally He is God. During this discussion time, let's think about a few references that relate to the humanity of Jesus.

1. Isaiah 7:14. About seven hundred fifty years before the birth of Jesus, Isaiah wrote that He would be born of a virgin. Why did the divine, eternal Christ become a man?

2. Matthew 1:1. What does the word *genealogy* mean? Who were two prominent ancestors of Jesus? What does this ancestral line tell us about Jesus?

3. Matthew 1:18–25. Who was the mother of Jesus? Did He have

a human father? What is another name for Jesus in this passage? What does it mean? Who became the husband of Mary?

4. Matthew 8:20. What do foxes and birds have that Jesus did not have when He lived on the earth? How did Christ identify with humanity during His ministry?

5. Matthew 9:6–13. Where was Jesus when He ate with "publicans and sinners"? How did that dinner show Christ's humanity? How did Jesus relate to the guests?

6. Matthew 9:35–37. Describe the ministry of Jesus. How did Jesus feel when He saw scattered people? Do the helpless, the lonely, the sick, and the persecuted have grounds for trusting Jesus today?

7. Matthew 26:36–45. What did the disciples do while Christ prayed in Gethsemane? How did that experience reveal the humanity of Jesus?

8. Mark 15:34–37. What question did Christ ask from the cross that demonstrated His humanity? How did His death show that He was a human being?

9. Luke 2:40–47. How does verse 40 verify His humanity? What about when He remained in Jerusalem to talk with the teachers? Tell what you see in these verses about both His humanity and His deity.

10. 1 John 1:1–4; 4:2–3. What did John write about Jesus that proved His humanity? Who witnesses to the fact that Jesus came to earth in the flesh? What does John say about Jesus (21:25) that proves He is the greatest man in history?

Jesus Christ— His Deity

48

Someone asked the writer Shalom Ash, who came to the U.S. from Poland in 1905, how he could write a book about Jesus, entitled *The Nazarene*. Mr. Ash, a Jew, responded by saying that he had read books from notable authors from the earliest times and had known many great writers of his generation, but he had never met or known about anyone as great as Jesus, whom many call the Christ.

Who is Jesus? The evangelical world believes that Jesus is God come in the flesh. Jesus is fully human as well as fully divine. John 1:1 states that Jesus is the Word and He is God. He is not "a god," but God incarnate. John 4:24 says that God is Spirit—not "a spirit," but Spirit. The Bible establishes this truth. How do we relate to Jesus? Calvin Miller (author, pastor, and professor) said that we should be "captive to Christ's lordship." Let's look at a few Scriptures that declare Christ is God as well as man.

1. Isaiah 9:6–7. What does the title Mighty God mean? How do the titles Prince of Peace and Everlasting Father refer to Christ's deity? (See 1 John 5:10–12.)

2. Micah 5:2. About seven hundred fifty years before Jesus' birth, Micah wrote that Jesus would be born in Bethlehem. And

though a babe, His origins are from ancient times—because He is eternal.

3. Luke 22:66–71; 23:1-5. What did the religious leaders ask Jesus? Who did He confess that He was? How did they feel about Jesus? What immediately followed?

4. John 1:1–2. What does "the beginning" mean in this passage? How can Christ as the Word be defined? What partnership does Jesus have with God?

5. John 1:29–34. What testimony did John the Baptist give about Jesus? What did He say about "the Lamb of God"? In verse 34, how did the baptizer identify Jesus?

6. John 8:23–24, 42, 56–58. Why did Jesus say that He is from above and not from the earth? Why should we believe? What did Jesus say about Abraham?

7. John 10:30, 34–39. How did Jesus identify himself with God? What does it mean when He says the Father is in Him and He is in the Father? Why did a conflict erupt between Jesus and the religious leaders?

8. Colossians 2:9–10. What does this verse say about the fullness of God in Christ? If Jesus is the head over every power and authority, what does that make Him?

9. Hebrews 1:1–4. How did God first speak to His people? In these last days, how has God spoken? How do these verses describe Jesus as God's final revelation?

10. Revelation 1:8; 17:14; 19:16. The Bible states that the Lord God is the Alpha and Omega and the Lord of Lords and King of Kings. Why does Jesus have these titles? (Isaiah 44:6; 45:18).

Jesus Christ— His Death

49

History records the deaths of philosophers, scientists, soldiers, inventors, politicians, teachers, religious leaders, and other prominent people. The death of Jesus Christ forever holds first place among all those who have died over the centuries. Anyone who tries to deny the birth and death of Jesus overlooks the plain facts of the Bible and human history. The Bible presents the case of the death of Jesus over and over again. The Old Testament prophesied Christ's death. Christ told of His coming death. The New Testament has indisputable evidence of the preexistence, virgin birth, sinless life, miracles, death, ascension, lordship, and return of Jesus Christ. Let's review some of the scriptural evidence that Christ died so that all who repent and believe in Him as their Savior might have everlasting life.

1. Isaiah 53:5–8. Isaiah states that Christ was pierced and crushed for our sins. He was led as a sheep to the slaughter (Acts 8:26–35). Why do you believe Jesus died?

2. Zechariah 12:10–12. How does this text describe the death of Jesus? How did the people in Jerusalem react to Christ's death? How do you feel about His death?

3. Matthew 20:17–19. What did Jesus tell His disciples on their way to Jerusalem? What were the Gentiles going to do with Him? How do you think the apostles thought and felt about this news? Shocked? In denial? Thinking He was talking about someone else?

4. Matthew 27:35–50. While Christ was being crucified, what did some say or shout to Him? What were His words in a loud voice just before He died? Why are the words in verse 50 significant?

5. Luke 22:19–20. What did Jesus teach His apostles about His death at the Last Supper? What did the bread represent? What did the wine represent?

6. Luke 24:44–46. What did Jesus say about the prophecies concerning His death? What Old Testament books contain these prophecies? Why do you think He was trying to prepare His disciples for these events?

7. John 19:38–42. Who gave permission for the body of Jesus to be taken down from the cross? What two men prepared Jesus' body for burial and placed Him in the new tomb?

8. Acts 2:22–23. Who spoke the words of this text? Why did the death of Jesus not come as a surprise to God? How did the condemnation and death of Jesus come about?

9. Hebrews 7:24–27; 9:20; 10:12. How is Jesus identified in the first passage? What kind of sacrifice did He make and for whom? Why is Christ's priesthood eternal? Will there ever be another sacrifice for sin?

10. 1 Peter 3:18. What does the phrase "the righteous for the unrighteous" (the just for the unjust) mean? What purpose for His death is stated in this passage? What happened after His death to complete our redemption?

Jesus Christ— His Resurrection

50

An ancient legend tells of a bird called the *phoenix*. According to the legend, the bird lives to be five hundred years old. When he dies, flames devour his body, and from the ashes another phoenix comes forth and repeats the process.

The resurrection of Jesus, on the other hand, is not a legend. The stories of Jesus are fact, not fiction. Let's look at what the Bible states as infallible proof of the resurrection. Acts 1:3–4 shows that Christ arose from the dead in his physical, immortal body after His crucifixion. Acts 1:3 is the only verse in the King James Version of the Bible that uses the word *infallible*.

1. Psalm 16:9–10; Acts 13:28–35. What is the significance of the promise that Jesus' body would not see corruption or decay? What happened after His resurrection to further assure His disciples that He was alive?

2. Matthew 12:40. How did Jesus relate the story of Jonah to His own resurrection? How did Jesus know that He would be raised from the dead following His crucifixion?

3. Matthew 28:1–15. What women arrived at the place of Christ's

burial? What did an angel show them? Who soon greeted them? Why were Roman soldiers bribed?

4. Luke 24:13–32. Who walked sadly along the road to Emmaus on the day of Christ's resurrection? How did Christ show them that He was alive? What did they say?

5. John 2:18–22. What did the Jews want Jesus to do to prove His authority? How did they misunderstand His words? When did the disciples remember those words?

6. John 20:19–28. Where did ten of the disciples meet on the Sunday evening after Christ's resurrection? How did Jesus appear to them and what did He do?

7. Acts 1:3. How many infallible proofs of Christ's resurrection can you name? New Testament believers had full evidence of Christ's resurrection. Why do some still doubt?

8. Acts 2:29–32. Who wrote about the resurrection of Jesus in Psalm 16? What happened to Christ's body? Who were witnesses of Christ's resurrection?

9. 1 Corinthians 15:1–8. Paul said that Christ died, was buried, and arose from the grave. Who were some who saw the resurrected Christ? How many saw Christ at one time?

10. Revelation 1:17–18. John saw Jesus about sixty years after His ascension. Why did Jesus tell John not to be afraid? Should we be afraid of death? Why or why not?

Jesus Christ—
His Return

51

More than two thousand years ago, Jesus came to this earth as the Son of God. He also received the title Son of Man because He was born of the Virgin Mary. Jesus came in fulfillment of many Old Testament prophecies.

The Bible says Jesus is going to come again. Dozens of references in both the Old and New Testaments state clearly that Jesus will return. Just as people in the first century did not understand everything about His first coming, in similar fashion we do not know everything about Christ's return. Charts and graphs and prophetic preaching do not agree on all the details of Christ's second coming. One fact is clear: Jesus will return. Let's look at a few biblical references about His return.

1. Daniel 7:13–14. In Daniel's vision of Christ's return, how did he see Him come? What will Jesus receive when He returns? How can we prepare for Christ's coming?

2. Matthew 24:29–31. When did Jesus say He would return? Why will the nations mourn? Who will gather the elect from the four winds?

3. John 14:1–3. What does Jesus describe that awaits believers in heaven? What other promise does He make?

4. Acts 1:7–11. Just before He ascended into heaven, what did Jesus say would happen? What did the two angels say to the men as they stood gazing into the sky?

5. Acts 3:19, 21. How can people prepare for Christ's return? What will be restored when He comes again?

6. 1 Corinthians 4:5. Why should we be careful about judging others before Christ returns? What dual work will Jesus do when He returns that may surprise us?

7. 1 Corinthians 15:24–26. To whom does Christ hand over the kingdom upon His return? What final enemy will be destroyed?

8. 1 Thessalonians 3:13. What was Paul's prayer? Is it being fulfilled? Who was Enoch? (Genesis 5:24; Jude 1:14). What did he prophesy?

9. 1 Thessalonians 4:16–17. What happens to the bodies of believers who have died before Christ returns? What happens to the living believers or saints when He comes?

10. 1 John 3:2. What is the meaning of the statement that we will be like Jesus when He returns? Are we ready to meet Him?

Joy

52

Everyone wants to be happy. People spend inordinate amounts of money on houses, cars, vacations, because they hope that these things will bring them real happiness. God wants us to have joy, which is far more than an emotional frenzy. Happiness depends on circumstance; God's joy comes about through a personal relationship with Jesus Christ. As Christians, we should let the joy of the Lord fill us. Heaven will be a place of eternal joy. More than five hundred verses of Scripture mention joy, which is the reality of total well-being based on our relationship with the Lord. Consider these ten Bible references that relate to joy:

1. Nehemiah 8:10. After rebuilding the walls of Jerusalem, Nehemiah told the Hebrews to celebrate with food and drink. (Some things never change.) What gave them strength? What can give us strength?

2. Psalm 51:12. Why did David ask God to restore the joy of his salvation? How does a person lose joy? What's the route to restoring joy? How does salvation give joy?

3. Proverbs 23:24–25. What happens in the life of a man who has a righteous son? How does a father feel about a wise son? Do you give your parents reason to be glad?

4. Isaiah 61:10. Do you think believers should be joyful or sad? What are some awesome benefits of those who trust in God? How does Isaiah describe what it is like to be clothed with God's salvation?

5. Jeremiah 15:16. What did the prophet do with God's Word? What does eating the Word mean? What blessing can a person have who fills his life with the Scriptures?

6. Habakkuk 3:15–18. What kind of tough times did Habakkuk and others face in their day? What reaction did Habakkuk have to calamity? What is a more common response to difficulties?

7. Luke 24:48–53. What did Jesus do forty days after His resurrection? Who was with Him? How did the disciples feel and what did they do?

8. 1 Peter 1:8. What is the typical reaction of believers to Jesus, even though they have not seen Him? How is Christian joy described? Can you say that you have this joy?

9. 3 John 1:3–4. What did the apostle John say caused him to greatly rejoice? What brings great joy to a parent or spiritual leader? What is truth? Explain or describe.

10. Jude 1:24. What did Jude say Jesus would do when He returns? What will be our prevailing emotion at that time? Give two reasons for this response.

Judging— Judgment

53

The book of Judges in the Old Testament tells about the life of Israel between when the Hebrew people left their wilderness wanderings and the time of their kings (c.1350–1000 BC). God gave His people a number of judges to help guide and protect them because most were forgetting God and living however they wanted to live.

Today most nations have a court system with a judge and jury to help keep order in society. We all face the temptation to be judges—we want to tell everyone else how to live. The Bible says a lot about judging and being judgmental. Let's check up on ourselves in this vital area of judgment and judging.

1. Matthew 7:1–5. When we set ourselves up as judge, what can happen? What must happen first, before we point out someone else's flaw? How does this Scripture relate to 1 Corinthians 2:15?

2. John 5:22; 18:28–32. Who has the authority to judge and why? Why did Jewish leaders take Jesus to Pilate, the Roman governor? Was anyone qualified to judge Jesus?

3. Acts 10:42. Who ordained or authorized Jesus to be the judge

of the living and the dead? How does Jesus' power as a judge relate to preaching?

4. Romans 2:1–3. What happens to the one who judges another? If we judge others while we do the same things as they do, what will God do with us?

5. Romans 14:4, 10–13. Why aren't we qualified to judge others? Where will we all appear one day? What will everyone do whether they want to or not? What do we put in another's way when we judge them?

6. 1 Corinthians 6:1–8. Why do Christians sometimes go to civil courts to settle problems among themselves? What did Paul say about such decisions? What does Paul suggest for solving disputes?

7. 2 Corinthians 5:10. What is the judgment seat of Christ? What will be the basis of rewards? What will we receive for the things done while in the body, good or bad? (1 Corinthians 3:13–15).

8. Colossians 2:16–17. How should we react to judgment from others concerning what we eat or drink or with regard to special days? What does Paul call these things in verse 17, and where is reality found?

9. James 4:11–12. When we speak against another person or judge another, what are we condemning? What is the one Lawgiver and Judge able to do? How does this fact rebuke us?

10. Revelation 20:11–12. Who did John see standing before the great white throne? What books were opened? In what way is each person judged before the Lord?

Justify— Justification

54

Justification is one of the more difficult words in the New Testament to understand. Some have tried to simplify the word by stating that justification means "just as if I had never sinned." Although this definition can be helpful, justification actually means "to make or declare righteous." Through faith in Christ, God declares us just, or redeemed. Can man by his works make himself right with God? Does justification come by faith and works? How is one justified? Let's see what the Bible says about justification.

1. Genesis 15:6. Moses says that Abraham believed God and that his belief was counted as righteousness. What is the object of our belief? That tells us how our belief can count as righteousness.

2. Job 25:4–6. Job had a valid question. How can a man be righteous before God? Is our so-called goodness enough? If the stars are impure in God's sight, what about man? Who has intervened for us to make righteousness possible?

3. Luke 16:13–15. Many Pharisees and Sadducees hated Jesus. How did these religious leaders justify themselves in the eyes of others?

4. Acts 13:38–39. Paul states that forgiveness and justification is only through Christ. Why can't the Law of Moses or man's good works make a person right before God?

5. Romans 3:19–26. What does the law do (verse 20)? What do the Law and Prophets say about God's righteousness? What is the only way that justification comes?

6. Romans 5:1–2. What does justification bring into one's life? Will faith in a religious system or a modern-day religious leader save anyone? Who gives us access to grace? What does the believer rejoice in?

7. Galatians 3:6–14, 19–29. How was Abraham justified? What is the purpose of the law? Since we can only be justified in God's sight by faith in Jesus Christ, what must we do?

8. Ephesians 2:8–9. How is anyone saved? Why can't a person be saved by his or her good works? How should people live who have received God's gift of salvation?

9. Titus 3:4–7. On what basis could God save us? Do good works have any merit? (Matthew 5:16). Discuss this among yourselves.

10. James 2:24–25. Does this Scripture contradict other verses that tell us about Abraham's justification? How did Abraham prove his faith by his works? Talk about how works validate our faith.

Kingdom of God

55

The basic meaning of *kingdom* is the territory over which a king rules. A kingdom is often thought of as a nation or country. God rules with authority in His kingdom, even though struggles continue among us. Several of Christ's parables relate to God's kingdom. When Jesus comes again, man's worldly kingdoms will come to an end, the devil's works will be shut down, and God will do everything according to His original plan (1 Corinthians 15:24). We should not be overly concerned about the details of when and how God will take final control of the world's empires. Jesus told His disciples that they didn't need to know "the times or dates the Father has set by His own authority" (Acts 1:7 NIV). Our main task is to witness in the power of the Holy Spirit. An excellent insight is given of God's kingdom in Romans 14:17: "The kingdom of God is not a matter of eating and drinking, but of righteousness, peace and joy in the Holy Spirit" (NIV). Look at some Scriptures that deal with God's kingdom:

1. Exodus 19:6. What plan did God have for the ancient Israelites when He called them? Do Christians inherit that responsibility? (1 Peter 2:5; Revelation 1:6).

2. 1 Chronicles 29:10–14. Discuss David's prayer. What did he

say about God? Who is the head of God's kingdom? How does David say we can share in the kingdom?

3. Daniel 2:44. What kind of kingdom is God setting up? What will happen to all worldly kingdoms or governments one day? When will this change take place?

4. Matthew 25:31–46. Who are those who will inherit the kingdom of God? Why will many not inherit that eternal kingdom? What message does Jesus have for us?

5. Luke 9:57–62. What did some would-be followers of Jesus hear Him say? How did some respond to Jesus? What did Jesus say to those who looked back?

6. Luke 17:20–21. How does the kingdom *not* come? Where is the kingdom of God? How would you interpret that? Does God rule over your life as King today? In what ways is this true?

7. John 3:3, 7. If one wants to see the kingdom of God, what must happen first? What is necessary for a person to enter the kingdom of God?

8. John 18:36–37. What did Jesus mean when He said His kingdom was not of this world? What would have happened if His kingdom were of this world? How did Jesus answer Pilate's question about His being a king?

9. Hebrews 12:28. What kind of kingdom do the people of God inherit? What kind of response should we have for a place in His kingdom? How are we to worship the Lord?

10. Revelation 11:15. What will happen to the kingdom of this world when Jesus returns? What is the response in heaven?

Life—
Eternal Life

56

Three men talked about what they would like people to say about them at their funerals. The first said he would like people to say that he had been a hardworking man, that he had been a good husband and father, and that everyone hated to lose him as their friend. The second one had a similar story. He wanted people to say that he was honest, had been going to church, and had been a role model family man. The third man just wanted someone at his funeral to suddenly exclaim, "Look! He's breathing!"

This thought-provoking study looks at a spiritual life that "keeps breathing." We can learn from the Scriptures that we don't have to die—with Christ in our lives we will live forever. Hopefully through what the Bible teaches we can all have a greater appreciation of the spiritual life that each of us receives through faith in Jesus Christ.

1. Genesis 2:7. When God created man, he became a living soul. What did God do to give life to the clod of dirt? How is God still our Life Sustainer?

2. Matthew 7:13–14. What kind of road leads to eternal life? What road leads to destruction and death? What gate do most people enter? Why is that true? Are both ways open to everyone?

3. Luke 18:28–30. What will people receive because of their commitment to Jesus? What have you left behind in order to follow Him? What reward is the greatest gift to those who believe in Jesus and follow Him?

4. John 5:24. What does it mean to hear Christ's words? What has to happen beyond hearing the Word? What do we escape by believing?

5. John 10:10–11. What purposes does a thief have in mind? What is Jesus' purpose toward us? Describe the abundant life. Like a good shepherd, what did Christ do to rescue us?

6. John 10:27–30. If we listen to His voice and follow Him, what does Christ promise? How secure are we in God's hands? What does Jesus remind us of in verse 30?

7. Colossians 3:1–4. If we have life in Christ, where should our interests lie? Comment on the hidden life with Christ. What will happen when Jesus returns?

8. 2 Timothy 1:8–10. What does Paul ask Timothy (and us) to do? How far back does the gift of grace go? What did Jesus bring with Him at His appearing and what has He accomplished for us through His death?

9. 1 John 5:9–13. What is God's testimony about Jesus? If we accept man's testimony, how much more ought we to believe what God says? How does God give us eternal life? What is the simple, straightforward statement about life in verse 12?

10. Revelation 21:25–27; 22:14, 17, 19. What are verses 25–27 speaking of? What are the qualifications for entering this city? Who calls us to enter and drink of the Water of Life? Is your name written in the Lamb's Book of Life?

Love— 1 Corinthians 13

57

Many years ago, Professor Henry Drummond of Oxford University became a believer after hearing evangelist Dwight L. Moody preach in a crusade in London. Dr. Drummond left his teaching post at the university and began to tell everyone what Christ had done for him. Later he wrote a book on 1 Corinthians 13 entitled *The Greatest Thing in the World*. Examine these revolutionary verses in the "love chapter" (NIV):

1. 1 Corinthians 13:1. What instruments are the metaphors for those who speak eloquently but without love? What is the effect of unrefined noise?

2. 1 Corinthians 13:2. What is a person like who has the gift of prophecy and has a full quota of wisdom, but lacks love? What about a faith that can move mountains?

3. 1 Corinthians 13:3. If anyone gives generously to the poor and is willing to sacrifice his or her body for a cause but does not have love, what does he or she gain?

4. 1 Corinthians 13:4. What words in verse 4 describe love? Talk

about these qualities of love and how they play out in a life. Which one of these qualities is weakest or strongest in your life?

5. 1 Corinthians 13:5–7. Love expresses itself in what kind of actions? Is there an expression in this list more important than another?

6. 1 Corinthians 13:8. How long does love last? What about other things that in life and in the church seem important to us? Who came as the full embodiment or expression of love? How did Jesus show that love?

7. 1 Corinthians 13:9–12. What are some noble qualities in our present life that lose their value when compared to love and life that are eternal? Like a child who matures, we will come to know fully the love of God. What we see now is but a poor reflection. Meditate on these things or discuss them in your group.

8. 1 Corinthians 13:13. Name three qualities of the Christian life that have significance. Why do you think these virtues or aspects of life are important?

9. 1 Corinthians 13:13. Why do you think love is greater than faith and hope? Does the fact that love is supreme reduce the value of faith and hope? Why?

10. 1 Corinthians 13:1–13. Do you think your life would change by reviewing this chapter each day for a week or a month? Will you try this experiment?

Love

There was a boy who made a trip across town every Sunday to attend a church. When he was asked why he made the long trip to be in that particular church, he answered, "Because they love little boys like me over there."

The Bible mentions love hundreds of times. Genuine love is the glue that holds husbands and wives together and constitutes a wonder-filled family for children and adults alike. When a person loves his or her country, it means he or she is concerned for that nation's health and well-being. When we love God as we should, we are on the road to royal living. Paul says that love is the greatest mark of a Christian. Look at these references to love as you discuss this fascinating topic:

1. Deuteronomy 6:5–6. What are the first attention-getting words in this Scripture? How are we to love God? How do we prove or show that we love God?

2. 1 Samuel 18:1–4. King Saul hated David. His son Jonathan loved him. How did he show his love for David? How can we show our love for others?

3. Isaiah 38:17. Even suffering can be for our good. How did God show His love for Isaiah and for Israel? What has God kept you

from? What has God done with our sins? How can we show our gratitude to God for His love and forgiveness?

4. Matthew 5:44-45. Who does Jesus say we are to love? How can we show our love even when it is difficult to do so? What kind of evidence do we have that we are all in this together?

5. Luke 10:25–37. What did a teacher of the law ask Jesus? What answer did he hear? Jesus often answered questions with questions. Looks like the teacher knew more than he thought! Jesus also answered questions with stories. What do you think of the illustration that Jesus gave about one's neighbor?

6. John 3:16. Who spoke these words? What did God do to show His love? When can a person claim this promise? What if a person rejects this promise of eternal life?

7. John 13:34–35. What new commandment did Jesus give His followers? What kind of love is Jesus talking about here? What is the result when we love one another? Is it easy to practice these words?

8. John 21:15–17. How many times did Jesus ask Simon Peter if he loved Him? What was Peter's response? Does this remind you of another time Peter gave three responses? What will we do if we love Jesus?

9. 1 Thessalonians 3:12. What does it mean to make love increase? If love overflows, what will be the result in family, church, community, and international life? Love is a "commodity" that spreads and increases as we practice it!

10. 1 Peter 4:8. What is the best quality of life? What does it mean to have fervent love for one another? How does love cover a multitude of sins?

Memory— Remember

59

Some scientific investigations have shown that goldfish have a memory span of three seconds. Praise the Lord that He made us with a memory that outdistances that beautiful fish. You and I remember many experiences from childhood to the present—our parents, work, school, friends, and much more. Did you ever have difficulties with your memory during test times? Some memories are wonderful, and some may be a nightmare. The Bible often tells us to remember.

1. Genesis 41:9–13. What did Pharaoh's chief cupbearer tell him? Who was the young Hebrew who interpreted their dreams? Why should we remember those who do favors for us? Why should we remember God's goodness to us?

2. Numbers 15:38–40. God gave clothing assignments to Israel's priests. Why did they have tassels on their clothes? What can we do to remember God's commandments?

3. Psalm 63:5–8. What is satisfying praise compared to? Where does the psalmist remember God? How comforting is this image of the believer and his God? Does this picture remind you of being loved as a child? How sweet the memory.

4. Proverbs 10:7. Why is the memory of a righteous person a blessing? When do we most remember them? Look at the contrast with the memory of an evil person. Is his name remembered?

5. Ecclesiastes 12:1. When is the best time to remember our Creator? Why? How do we keep God at the center of our thoughts? Why is this important?

6. Jonah 2:7. Where was Jonah when he prayed? When did he remember God? What action did he take? Why do some people wait until they are in trouble or dying to remember God?

7. Zechariah 10:9. Who is Zechariah talking about? God said He would chasten His people by sending them into faraway countries because of their sin. What would they do then? What will it take for us to remember God?

8. Matthew 26:6–13. Why was the woman in this text being criticized? By whom? What did Jesus say about her actions? (Motive is everything.) What did Jesus say would be remembered throughout the world along with the gospel?

9. Luke 22:12–20. When and where did the Last Supper take place? Why was it called the Last Supper? What did Jesus say about it? What did the bread and wine represent? What are we remembering when we celebrate the Lord's Supper? Why is this important?

10. Hebrews 13:1–3. What benefit may come to those who entertain strangers? How can we remember those in prison and those who are mistreated? What are some of the unconventional ways people end up in prison today? How might we remember them?

Mercy

60

To enlarge your concept of mercy, study Exodus 25:10–22. When Israel came out of Egypt, God asked them to build a tabernacle where His people could worship. The ark of the covenant was placed inside the Holy of Holies. The ark was about the size of a church Communion table. The Ten Commandments were kept inside the ark, giving it the name *ark of the covenant.* Once a year the Great High Priest sprinkled blood on the covering of the ark, signifying that the sins of the people had been covered. The ark's top, or lid, was called God's mercy seat because He showed mercy to His people when He saw the blood. God's mercy is mentioned 148 times in the Old Testament and various times in the New Testament. Praise the Lord for His mercy!

1. Nehemiah 9:19–21. God blessed Israel for forty years in the desert. Did God provide the necessities of life? How does He show His mercy now?

2. Proverbs 28:13. What happens to one who refuses to confess his sin? How does God show mercy to those who admit their wrongs? Is confession an easy experience? Is it harder to confess your sins to God or to people you have sinned against?

3. Lamentations 3:21–23. What gives us hope? How is the fact that

His mercies are new every morning a great comfort? How are God's mercies life-sustaining?

4. Micah 7:18. How does this verse surprise you? Who may receive God's mercies? How does God feel about showing mercy to us?

5. Luke 10:35–37. This text concludes the story of the Good Samaritan. Is mercy part of a creed or is it intended to be practiced? How does this Scripture illustrate true mercy, going the extra mile? Where and how can we show mercy?

6. Romans 12:1. God calls His people to live consecrated lives. How is this offering an act of worship? Without God's mercy could we live for His glory?

7. Romans 12:8. Mercy is a gift from God. How can we cultivate this gift? How does showing mercy cheerfully contribute to the effectiveness of the gift?

8. Ephesians 2:4–5. What three attributes of God have brought us salvation? Name times in your life when God has been merciful to you.

9. Titus 3:4–6. How are we saved? Do our righteous deeds figure in to the equation? Through what two attributes of God are we shown mercy?

10. Hebrews 2:17; 4:16. What made Jesus the merciful High Priest in service to God? What did this service include? Where must we go to receive God's mercy? With what attitude?

Miracles

61

One day Jesus and His apostles got in a boat to cross the Sea of Galilee. He soon fell asleep, and then a powerful storm came up and the boat started filling with water. The apostles called out to Jesus and He stopped the storm. Then they asked, "Who is this? Even the wind and the waves obey him!" (Mark 4:41 NIV). Jesus healed the sick, raised the dead, and fed hungry multitudes so that people would believe in Him. God performed dozens of miracles through Moses, Elijah, Elisha, Peter, and Paul. Although skeptics today question miracles, Bible miracles are never exaggerated.

The Bible warns of false prophets and fake miracles (Matthew 7:22–23). At the same time, God's Word tells of genuine wonders (*terata*), powers (*dunameis*), and signs (*semeia*). (See Hebrews 2:4.) When we allow God to step into our lives and bring about a change that glorifies Him, that's a miracle! God still creates miracles through His people. The following references give insight into the supernatural actions of God:

1. Genesis 1:1. The Hubble Space Telescope has shown us two galaxies, 114 million light years in space. Was creation an accident, or was it the plan of God?

2. Exodus 14:21–28. When Moses stretched out his hand in obedience to God, what happened? Do you think it took faith for the Hebrews (Israelites) to walk through the pathway in the sea? What happens to those who mock God and persecute His people?

3. Daniel 3:9–27. Why did Nebuchadnezzar have three young Hebrew men thrown into a fiery furnace? How does their testimony to the king speak of their deep faith in the sovereignty of God? Who appeared with them in the fire? What marks did they bear for having been through the fire?

4. Matthew 28:1–13. What did an angel tell Mary Magdalene and the other Mary? What did the resurrected Savior say to them? How did some Jewish leaders react?

5. Mark 1:21–28. Who came to a synagogue in Capernaum while Jesus was there? What did the man say to Jesus? How did Jesus respond? What amazed the people?

6. Luke 1:35–37. What did the angel say the Holy Spirit would do? Who besides Mary would experience a miraculous birth? How do we know this is true (verse 37)?

7. Luke 17:11–19. What illness did the men have who cried out to Jesus? What did He tell them to do? When did the healing take place? How did they respond? Do we sometimes take for granted God's healing grace and power?

8. John 3:1–3. Nicodemus acknowledges that Jesus has come from God. What do you think of Jesus' response? What does *born again* mean? Would you consider this a miracle? Have you experienced this?

9. John 9:1–11. What did Jesus' disciples ask Him when they came upon the blind man? What was Jesus' answer? How was he healed? Why didn't Jesus just pray for the man and heal him on the spot? What kind of response did the man get from the neighbors? Can miracles happen today?

10. Acts 3:1–16. Tell about the man who had been lame from birth. Whom did Peter credit with the miracle even though *he* had declared the man's healing? What other miracle did Peter speak of in verse 15?

Music— Singing

The word *music* comes from the word *muse,* which means "to meditate" or "become absorbed in thought." Music generally refers to pleasing sounds and harmony.

As we sing hymns of praise, we remember who God is and honor Him with our singing and playing musical instruments. Does music in our churches sometimes appeal to worldly ways? Is music in your church worshipful? Heartwarming? Christ-honoring? Scripturally accurate? Spiritually uplifting? Are the words easily understood and remembered? Consider some Bible references about music and song:

1. Genesis 4:21. Who was the inventor of music? What are the first two musical instruments mentioned in the Bible? How does a person become a musician?

2. Exodus 15:1–18. Israel sang a song of praise to God. What does this chapter teach about God, His enemies, and His people? What can hymns and choruses teach us?

3. Job 29:11–14. The patriarch Job defended his life by saying that he helped the poor, the widows, and the dying sing for joy. How do we put a song of praise in the lives of others?

4. Psalm 104:33. This is a good verse to memorize. How long should we sing to the Lord? Have you praised God in song today? Why is praise beneficial to all concerned? Share some experiences.

5. Psalm 145:1–7. According to this psalm, what are some reasons for singing to the Lord? What does it mean to joyfully sing of God's righteousness?

6. Isaiah 35:1–10. Is there power in praise and song? Who should be helped by us, according to this passage? How does the prophet describe our pilgrimage to Zion or to heaven? How should our pilgrimage end? Will it ever end?

7. Zephaniah 3:17. How does God feel about His people? What do you think about God singing over you? Have you ever listened to one of His solos sung just for you?

8. Matthew 26:26–30. It is interesting to read what the disciples did after they shared the Last Supper with their Lord (verse 30). What do you think they sang? Where did they go after the hymn?

9. Ephesians 5:19–20. How do we communicate by singing? Are our songs spiritual? Is the message understood? In what ways does our singing glorify the Lord?

10. Revelation 15:3. What does the song of Moses and the Lamb tell about Moses and God's people? What are the words of the song of the Lamb (verse 3)?

Patience

We have all heard the expression "the patience of Job." The original definition of *patience* was "to stay beneath a load without letting the knees buckle." The Greek word is *upomeno*. *Upo* is a prefix meaning "under." *Meno* means "abide or remain." What is your experience with patience? Look at these Scripture passages that deal with the virtue of patience:

1. Psalm 40:1–3. What does it mean to wait patiently on the Lord? Can you share an experience like David's? What are a few good results from waiting on the Lord?

2. Isaiah 30:18. How do you feel as you wait for God to be compassionate? Is it easy to run ahead of God? How are we blessed if we wait for God to act?

3. Matthew 18:23–35. Study this account of two debtors. What did the first one ask his master to do? Then what did that servant turn around and do? Do these stories in any way apply to us? If yes, in what ways?

4. Acts 26:1–3. While Paul was on trial, he asked King Agrippa to patiently hear him out. Do you sometimes wish people would

listen to you with patience? Why? Is it easy to listen to others patiently, or do we tend to interrupt and give our opinion?

5. Romans 15:5–6. Have you ever thought of the Lord as being the God of patience or endurance? How has God shown His patience with the world? With you? In what ways?

6. 1 Thessalonians 5:14. Why is it difficult to be patient with family members as well as others outside the family circle? Can we learn to be patient with everyone?

7. Hebrews 6:12. How is patience involved with our eternal inheritance? What about with temporary blessings?

8. Hebrews 12:1. What kind of race are we running every day? How do those in athletic events show patience? Explain. Why is patience needed for everyday living?

9. James 5:11. What Old Testament man is a stunning example of patience? Do friends like those in Job's circle ever test your faith? How?

10. 1 Peter 2:20. When are patience and endurance to be commended? Which is more difficult: to suffer for wrongdoing or to suffer when you do what is right? Explain.

Peace

64

In 1519, Ponce de Leon of Spain first looked across the mountains of Panama and saw a great body of water. Hardly a breeze was blowing and the ocean looked like a sea of glass. He called that body of water the Pacific Ocean because of its condition at the time. He didn't know that storms could explode across the water and that same vista would become anything but calm and peaceful.

We all want a peaceful life—and not just one that looks peaceful for the moment. God offers us in His Word the promise of peace if we will accept what is written.

1. Psalm 34:14. What do people search for in life? What does this Scripture say we should seek? How do we pursue peace? Is peace always possible?

2. Psalm 119:165. What is a prerequisite of peace in this verse? What is the reward of loving God's law?

3. Isaiah 26:3. What is the result of a steadfast mind? What does it mean to have the mind fixed on God? What else is involved in keeping centered on God?

4. Isaiah 48:18, 22. If people hear and obey God's commands, what

will be the result? According to verse 22, who does not have peace? Why is this true?

5. Luke 1:69–79. Who was the prophet who announced the coming of Jesus? What does Christ offer everyone? How are we guided into the path of peace?

6. John 14:27. What legacy did Christ promise His followers? What is the difference between Christ's peace and the peace of the world? What admonition closes the verse?

7. John 16:30–33. What things did Jesus share with His disciples (verse 32)? Why? In the face of trials, what should be our attitude? How is this possible?

8. Romans 12:18. What is Paul's admonition in this verse? On whom does he place the responsibility? Who does it include?

9. Ephesians 2:14–15. Who is our peace? What did Christ do to break down the barriers that divide us?

10. Philippians 4:7. What guards our hearts and minds in Christ? Can God's peace be fully comprehended? Do you think this is one reason why people have a hard time accepting God's peace? Why is it not possible to measure God's peace?

Pleasures

65

A boy walked up to a man and said, "I have a bird in my hand. Can you tell me if the bird is dead or alive?" The man waited a moment and answered, "That all depends. If I say he is dead, you may turn him loose and show me that the bird is very much alive. But if I say he is alive, you may suffocate the bird and he will be dead."

Sometimes there is no clear answer. For example, are pleasures right or wrong? That depends on what kind of pleasures we are talking about and how we handle them. The Bible shows that some pleasures are good and others are evil. Let's look at what we can learn about pleasures from God's Word.

1. Psalm 36:7–9. This verse speaks of a river of God's pleasures. With His unfailing love, what unending pleasures can we have with God?

2. Psalm 111:1–3. What are the works of the Lord in relation to creation? What about His work of redemption? We have reason to praise and extol His name for all His wonderful works. We can delight in God's creation.

3. Proverbs 21:17. What pleasures might this verse be referring to? Why might a person who loves wine and oil never be rich?

4. Isaiah 44:24–28. Does God have eventual control of rulers and nations? How do these verses assure us of God's power and control in the dealings of men? What about in things pertaining to our daily lives and comfort?

5. Isaiah 58:12–14. God promises certain things to those who honor the Sabbath. What rewards are mentioned here? How can we keep the Sabbath today?

6. Ezekiel 18:23, 32. Does God take any pleasure in the death of the wicked? What does please Him? What is the remedy for avoiding God's wrath (verse 32)?

7. Haggai 1:7–8, 12–14. What did God want His people to do? What promises did God make to them? How does God work with His people? Does God enjoy our success?

8. Luke 8:14. Who is represented by the seed sown among thorns? What chokes the life and growth from us? How can we relate to this parable today?

9. Luke 12:32. Why did Jesus tell His followers not to be afraid? What does He promise them as well as us? Do God's pleasures surprise you?

10. Revelation 4:11. God created the universe for His own purposes and pleasure. We praise Him as we enjoy all that He has created. What kinds of pleasures can we expect from God beyond this present life?

Poverty or Poor

David Brenner (b. 1871) came to the U.S. from a poverty-stricken background in Russia. In America, this sculptor became famous for engraving the face of Abraham Lincoln on our one-cent currency, the penny. President Lincoln said that God must love the poor, because He made so many of them. Jesus said that the poor will always be with us.

Nothing is inherently wrong with being poor or rich. The Bible says that God made both. Sometimes those who crusade on behalf of the poor have a lot of money themselves. We don't always practice what we preach. John Wesley is said never to have accumulated wealth because he gave away all the extra he received. How many imitate the example of the apostles who left all to follow Jesus?

Many wealthy people do give generously, while in some cases the poor don't make any effort to improve themselves, only waiting for handouts. Other poor people are stuck in poverty and can't find a way out. Natural disasters, war, disease, and a lack of jobs help bring on dire circumstances. Let's study what the Word says about poverty.

1. Exodus 23:11. Why were landowners told to allow their land to remain idle every seventh year? Discuss this ancient rule. What is the lesson in it?

2. Psalm 102:17. How does God respond to the prayers of the destitute? What does He think of the poor? Where can these people be found?

3. Proverbs 17:5; 19:17. How does the way we treat the poor relate to God? What happens to those who take advantage of a disaster? If we help the poor, how is that lending to God? How does the Lord repay the lender?

4. Isaiah 3:14–15. Who is guilty of crushing the poor? How is this done? Why should we feel responsible to others? What about other nations?

5. Jeremiah 22:13–19. How did some kings take advantage of the poor and oppressed? What does this passage say about Jehoiakim? How do people today take advantage of the poor or uninformed?

6. Amos 2:6–7. Who were the oppressors in this passage? Does this kind of oppression happen today? What is at the root of such behavior?

7. Matthew 19:21. What did Jesus tell a rich man to do? What kinds of treasures might this person have to give away? Should everyone follow this same route?

8. Romans 15:26–29. Since the Gentiles had benefited spiritually from the Jews, what did Paul challenge the Gentiles to do? With whom can we share materially?

9. 2 Corinthians 6:4–10. Among all the things the servants of God suffered in Paul's day, what does he mention in verse 10 that may surprise you? How do you make others rich if you have nothing? Is material wealth the only wealth to be considered?

10. 2 Corinthians 8:9. What was the status of Jesus before He came from heaven? How did He become poor? What did He do to help others? How can we enrich the lives of others?

Praise

Praise to the Lord can be expressed in words such as *thanksgiving, gratitude,* and *amen.* Praise in its various expressions appears more than three hundred times in the Bible. How much do we praise the Lord in our daily prayers? If we read through the book of Psalms, we might be astounded at the dozens of times the writers express praise to the Lord. At the same time, we should keep in mind that praise is an expression of thanks. When we say thank you to someone, they usually know to what we are referring. So in our praise, we should be specific and clear. Here are a few biblical references to praise:

1. Genesis 29:31–35. The fourth son of Jacob and Leah was named Judah, meaning "Praise the Lord." Who came from Judah's tribe?

2. 1 Chronicles 23:5. At the dedication of Solomon's temple, what group was matched to the number of gatekeepers? Does this give us an idea of the value Solomon placed on worship? How do we value worship times in the church?

3. 2 Chronicles 20:15–30. Why was King Jehoshaphat told not to be afraid when he faced his enemies? What did the king direct

his men to do (verse 21)? What happened to their enemies when the men began to praise the Lord?

4. Psalms 71:6–8; 119:62, 164. Do you frequently fill your mouth with praise to the Lord? What about midnight praises? Share some of your own praise experiences.

5. Psalms 148:1–150:6. Read, meditate, and comment on these three chapters of praise. How does almost everything praise the Lord?

6. Luke 1:57–64. Elizabeth and Zechariah had heard from the Lord and knew what their child's name should be. Struck dumb for his unbelief, what did Zechariah do when John was born? What do you think loosed his tongue? Do we praise the Lord when children are born?

7. Luke 19:28–40. How did Jesus' followers react to Jesus as He approached Jerusalem? What did the Pharisees say about it? How did Jesus respond to them?

8. Acts 3:1–8. What happened to a crippled man at the temple in Jerusalem? How was Peter's prayer/declaration unique? What did the man do when he was healed? What should be our response when Christ touches our lives?

9. Hebrews 13:15. What are we to offer God? Is there a limit to our praise? If we confess His name, what is the natural outcome?

10. Revelation 5:12–13. Who is worthy of all praise? Can you fathom the sound of every creature in heaven and earth and under the earth and in the sea giving praise to the Lord? What do you think praise will be like in heaven?

Prayer and Praying

A long time ago, before the battle of Edgehill in England, Sir John Astley lifted his hands toward heaven and prayed, "O Lord, you know how busy I must be this day; if I forget you, do not forget me." Then he arose from his knees and shouted to his troops, "March on, boys!"

God has a door open to His throne room that allows His people to pray or speak to Him at any time. Praying is the privilege of all believers. The Bible teaches about the amazing and awesome theme of prayer. Hopefully after this study on prayer, we will be more committed to prayer than ever before.

1. Deuteronomy 9:9, 18, 25–29. How long was Moses up on the mountain? How many times did he repeat his stay? What did he do there, and what did he ask God to do? When is extended prayer needed?

2. 1 Kings 18:36–39. Read the background story in verses 25–35. What did Elijah pray for and what was the result? What was the response of the people? Talk about the amazing things that have happened in our day when people prayed.

3. 2 Kings 19:17–20. Who threatened Israel? What did Hezekiah

and Isaiah ask God to do? What happened to Sennacherib (Isaiah 37:36–38)? What are some prerequisites to effective prayer?

4. Psalm 55:16–17. What did David say God did in response to his prayers? How often did David pray? What was the level of his prayers' intensity? Share a prayer experience you have had.

5. Isaiah 59:1–4. Is God capable of hearing and answering the prayers of His people? Why does God sometimes not hear our prayers? What can we do to ensure our prayers will be heard?

6. Matthew 6:6–7. Why did Jesus emphasize the importance of secret prayer? What does this Scripture teach about vain repetitions (babbling like pagans)? What about public prayers?

7. Matthew 21:13. Who identified God's house as a place of prayer? What had others made it to be? Is the church the only place to pray? Name some places to pray and ways to pray that may help us to better focus on God.

8. Luke 22:39–44. Upon reaching the garden, what did Jesus tell His disciples to do? Describe the prayer of Jesus in Gethsemane. Who strengthened Him as He struggled in prayer? Is it sometimes difficult to pray that God's will be done, especially when we know what that will is? Why or why not?

9. Philippians 4:6–7. What is the best prescription for worry? What is the result of making our requests to God? Why are we told to pray about everything?

10. Revelation 5:8. What was in the bowls the angels and elders offered before the Lamb? Are there prayers still to be answered?

Pride

69

One of Aesop's Fables tells about a farmer's daughter who was bringing a bucket of milk from the barn. She thought, "The money that I'll have after this milk is sold will buy 300 eggs. From these eggs, I can probably have 250 chickens. The chicks will grow fast so that by the end of the year when they're taken to the market, I can sell them and use the money to buy a new dress. Then I will go to Christmas parties where young fellows will propose to me, but I will refuse every one of them." At that moment, she tossed her head back with pride, the milk bucket fell to the ground, and all her imaginary plans crashed with it. Pride causes the small and the great to fall. Let's get a bird's-eye view of the pride that places a man in the center of his own little world.

1. Exodus 18:1-11. Jethro, the father-in-law of Moses, was delighted to learn of Pharaoh's defeat. What was the price of Pharaoh's pride? What does pride cost some today? Give some examples.

2. Leviticus 26:18–21. What happens when people stubbornly go their own way? What happens to the sky as a metaphor of unanswered prayer? How does a failure of crops relate to stubbornness and pride? To what degree are afflictions multiplied to the proud?

3. 1 Samuel 1:13–22. Hannah rejoiced over the birth of Samuel. She was proud of her son, but not arrogant. How did she give glory to God for hearing and answering her prayer? How can we follow her example?

4. Proverbs 16:5, 18. What attitudes precede a fall? What does our Lord think of the proud of heart? How does Genesis 11:1–9 illustrate the danger of pride? To what lengths did God go to see the plans of prideful man thwarted?

5. Jeremiah 13:15–19. What warning did Israel receive if they refused God's message? What was Jeremiah's response? How do we feel when people turn away from God?

6. Ezekiel 30:1–6. The prophet Ezekiel wrote about some of the allies of Egypt. Why did that nation's strength fail? What eventually happens to those who stand against God's people?

7. Daniel 4:28–37. What did Nebuchadnezzar say about Babylon? What happened to him as a result of God's judgment? What was his response after God restored him? What can we learn from Nebuchadnezzar's experience?

8. Luke 18:10–14. What was the prayer of the religious Pharisee? Do we sometimes pray about ourselves, letting God know our importance (as if He doesn't know us)? How does the prayer of the tax collector stand in direct contrast to that of the Pharisee? Who went home justified? Why is some praying ineffective?

9. 1 Timothy 3:1–7. What requirement for a deacon in the church relates to pride? What is the danger of pride in a church leader? How do these requirements apply to any believer?

10. 1 John 2:16. Why does Scripture warn us not to love the world? What do the words *pride of life* mean? (See also NIV.) What does 1 Peter 5:6 say about humility?

Prisons and Inmates

70

In the United States of America, more than one and a half million people are incarcerated in state and federal prisons. The majority are inmates because they have broken laws and committed crimes. Our prison system provides beds, entertainment, and food for those behind bars. A few are so pleased with their treatment that they would rather stay in prison than be set free. However, prison life has many negative features. I have spent a lot of time going to prisons for ministry, and for several years I have been writing to a prisoner that I have never met. The Bible challenges us to minister to those in prison.

1. Genesis 39:3–20. Joseph went to prison in Egypt because Potiphar's wife falsely accused him. Do you think prison inmates today have sometimes been falsely accused? Why or why not?

2. Judges 16:20–21, 25–30. What tragedy befell Samson when he lost his strength? Talk about the dangers, confinement, and loneliness of inmates.

3. Jeremiah 37:21; 38:6–13. Who was Jeremiah? Why was he sent to prison? Who saved him from death? Are there many Christians in prisons today? Talk about persecution and the fact that

many who speak for God around the world are imprisoned for their faith.

4. Matthew 11:1–4; 14:1–12. Why was John the Baptist in prison? What happened to him on Herod's birthday? What did Jesus say about him? (Matthew 11:7–12). Do Christ's followers escape hardships?

5. Matthew 25:34–40. What kind of prison ministry can we have today? What is promised those who minister to the hungry, the sick, or the imprisoned? Who are we ministering to when we serve others?

6. Luke 4:18–19 (Isaiah 61:1-2). What did Isaiah's anointing include? How can we help those who are in a prison of their own making, or who are bound by habits, wrong thinking, oppression, or other kinds of "chains"?

7. Luke 22:31–33. How did Simon Peter express his commitment to Christ? Do we sometimes make big commitments in the heat of emotion and later lose heart and renege on our promises?

8. Acts 16:20–34. Why were Paul and Silas in prison? What were they doing at midnight? What was their response to the jailer after the earthquake? How does this incident serve as an example of being ready to witness for Christ at any moment?

9. Ephesians 4:1. Paul was a prisoner in Caesarea for two years before his Roman jail time (Acts 24:25-27). What did he do in Rome? (Acts 23:11). Do we serve God where we are?

10. 2 Timothy 1:8. Paul was imprisoned in Rome between AD 61 and 63. His last incarceration was AD 67. How did he admonish Timothy when he wrote to him?

Promises

71

When a child does not behave, he or she may say to Mom or Dad, "Don't punish me this time; I'll never do it again." When people feel the pressures of life coming down on them, they may be ready to make all kinds of promises. We also like to hear promises, such as, "You're going to get a really great birthday present." Adults like to hear promises about job promotions, longer vacations, salary increases, or church growth. God promises that His Word will not return empty, but will accomplish the purpose for which it was sent. We find a lot of promises in the Bible with eternal benefits.

1. Genesis 28:20–22. What did Jacob expect God to do for him? What promises did he make to God? What are some practical promises we make to God?

2. Deuteronomy 9:25–29. What did Moses tell God people would say if He didn't keep His promise to take Israel into the Promised Land? How did he describe Israel (verse 29)?

3. 1 Kings 8:56. What did the Lord promise His people? How does the promise of rest relate to us? List some of God's promises that you want to see fulfilled in your life.

4. Acts 2:29–33. What promise did God give to David? Who sits on David's throne? What was promised to all of us upon Jesus' death (verse 33)?

5. Acts 2:36–39. When the Jews heard Peter say that the crucified Christ was Lord, what did they ask? What did Peter tell them to do? What gift would they receive?

6. Romans 4:18–22. What response did Abraham have to God's promise of a son? Why was that a monumental test for Abraham? Why should we believe God's promises in spite of circumstances?

7. Ephesians 6:1–3. What is the first commandment with a promise? How might parents have some part in seeing this promise fulfilled for their children?

8. Hebrews 6:13–15. What promises did God make to Abraham? When did Abraham obtain the promise? Name some promises God has made that are not yet fulfilled.

9. 2 Peter 1:3–4. What has the Lord provided for us by His divine power? What are some of the great and precious promises referred to here? How do we participate in the divine nature?

10. 1 John 2:25. What is the promise mentioned in this text? How may a person claim this promise?

Reconciliation

72

One of the many heart-touching stories in Genesis relates to Joseph and his brothers. Joseph's brothers had sold him into slavery. Thirteen years later, when the brothers made a trip to Egypt looking for food, they came before Joseph without knowing who he was. Finally Joseph revealed himself, embraced them, and wept profusely. The years of broken relationships were restored because Joseph took the steps necessary to bring about reconciliation.

Many people need to be reconciled to God as well as to others. God makes restoration possible with himself and with others through the gift of His Son Jesus. The offended Lord removes every hindrance from the broken relationship, but each person must accept the forgiveness that God offers. Reconciliation between Jew and Gentile, between family members, and between nations can take place if we go about it God's way. Will we do it?

1. Genesis 27:41–45; Genesis 32–33. Genesis tells about a broken relationship between Jacob and Esau. Did they become fully reconciled? In what ways do we face this problem today? What can we do about it?

2. Matthew 5:23–24. If two believers have a conflict, what should

they do before bringing an offering before God? How might churches be affected if members practiced this?

3. Acts 15:36–41. What problem erupted between Paul and Barnabas? How was the disagreement resolved? Is it always a bad thing to go our separate ways?

4. Romans 5:10–11. Even while some are enemies of God, how can they be reconciled? What blessings come through restored relationships?

5. 1 Corinthians 7:10–11. What does Paul say about separation and remarriage? What is the highest way to take, according to this passage?

6. 2 Corinthians 5:18–20. Who initiates and makes possible reconciliation with God? What work should the reconciled do? Why should there be urgency in this work?

7. Ephesians 2:14–18. What has Jesus done to reconcile Jews and Gentiles? How does reconciliation between people take place? Name some places or groups where reconciliation is needed.

8. Philippians 4:2–3. Who were Euodias and Syntyche? What appeal did Paul make to them? What would restored relationships between Christians bring about today?

9. Colossians 1:19–22. Who has reconciled us to God? What alienates us from God? How are personal relationships affected by sin? How can they be restored?

10. Philemon 1:8–19. Who did Paul love as a son? While in chains, he sent this former slave to help in the church and to represent him (Paul). How does Paul show his love for this young man and confidence that he will be received? How could this story apply to us?

Redemption 73

Several years ago an Exxon oil executive was captured by guerilla fighters in Cordoba, Argentina. The *montoneros* demanded several million dollars for the man's release. The company paid the ransom, or redemption price, for him.

Jesus paid a heavy price for mankind's redemption from sin and Satan. Through the years theologians have debated about how our redemption from the devil works. But regardless of the details, we know that Jesus came and on the cross paid the full price for our release. Let's study the Scriptures that explain some facts about our spiritual and physical redemption.

1. Ruth 4:1–12. By what transaction did Boaz become the kinsman-redeemer of Ruth? Why did he gather elders around him when he purchased the property and announced that Ruth would be his wife?

2. Job 19:25–27. What positive statement did Job make about his Redeemer? How did Job describe his future relationship with Jesus?

3. Psalm 130:7–8. Why should God's people place their hope in

the Lord? What will God do for Israel? What do you think about God's goodness to you?

4. Isaiah 51:11. Why will the ransomed of the Lord enter Zion with joy and singing? What will come to an end? Do you anticipate the joys of heaven?

5. Romans 3:23–24. Why do people need God's redemption? How do we know that everyone sins? How is humanity made right with God? Who makes our redemption possible?

6. Galatians 3:10–12. Does the law save? How did Christ redeem us from the law's curse? How do the blessings promised to Abraham and to Israel apply to Christians?

7. Titus 2:10–14. To whom has salvation appeared? What does redemption teach us? How eager are we to do what is good?

8. Hebrews 9:22, 25–28; 10:11–14. What does the law require for the cleansing of sin? Through whose sacrifice is mankind redeemed? How did Christ pay for man's sin? How is Christ's sacrifice different from the one priests offered repeatedly for sinners in the Old Testament?

9. 1 Peter 1:18–21. Why can't salvation be purchased? How long ago was our redemption secured? How did God seal our redemption after Christ's death?

10. Revelation 5:9. Who was worthy to take the scroll and open the seals? Is any people group excluded from redemption through the blood of Christ? What does our future hold after this life?

Repentance

74

Anyone who knows about military service understands marching orders. One command that those in basic military training frequently hear is "To the rear, march!" This means to turn around and go in the opposite direction. The biblical word *repentance* means to change the way one thinks and lives. From the spiritual and moral perspective, repentance means turning away from sin and turning to God. Repentance is the spiritual change that the Holy Spirit brings about in a person's life, causing him or her to become a new creation in Christ. The Bible mentions repentance more than one hundred times, calling for a reorientation of one's entire life and purpose. Consider the following Scriptures:

1. Genesis 6:5-7. *Repentance* in this text refers to God's grief over having made man. The fact that God wanted to "start over" gives a good picture of repentance. Discuss how sometimes people think they can be saved without repentance. Is this possible?

2. 1 Kings 8:46–51. Solomon prayed at the temple dedication with a strong plea for mercy for his people in response to true repentance. How does he identify them in verse 51? Do we tend to give reasons why we or others should be forgiven? What is the only true basis for forgiveness (on God's part and on our part)?

3. Job 42:6. Job admitted that he had said things without understanding. When Job saw the Lord, what did he do? How does repentance restore our fellowship with God?

4. Jeremiah 8:4–12. Man is sometimes like a horse charging into battle. He does not stop to think or change direction. How do these verses describe ancient Israel? Do they also describe us?

5. Ezekiel 14:6; 18:30, 32. God's prophets called for His people to turn from idolatry and detestable practices and return to God. Do these and other verses give us a picture of the strong theme of repentance that runs through the Bible? What changes in our lives do we need to make? How important is change at the right time?

6. Matthew 3:4–10. How did John the Baptist describe repentance? In spite of his strong voice and conviction, John was a humble man (verse 11). How seriously do people take their baptism today? What needs to accompany baptism?

7. Luke 13:1–5. What two tragic stories do we find in these verses? How did Jesus apply these stories to the urgent call to repentance? Is it ever too late to repent?

8. Acts 5:29–33. What message did Simon Peter preach? How did his presentation of Jesus—sent by God, raised up by God, seated with God—cause such a stir? Why did some respond to the message as they did? How should we?

9. Acts 17:22–30. Read carefully Paul's message that he preached at Mars' hill in Athens, Greece. What did he say about idols? What did he say God commands? Are there things in our lives that call for repentance?

10. 2 Peter 3:9–11. Since God does not want any person to die, what must everyone do in order to live? What event in the future requires that we be prepared?

Rest

75

This lighthearted poem, inscribed on a woman's tombstone, is an entertaining picture of what it means for some to be at rest: "Here lies an old woman who was always tired. She lived in a house where help was not hired. Her last words were: 'Dear friend, I am going where cooking ain't done, or mopping or sewing, but everything there is exact to my wishes, for where they don't eat, there's no washing of dishes. Don't mourn for me, don't mourn for me ever! I'm going to do nothing forever and ever!'" Sometimes we want rest from the burdens and responsibilities of life. The Bible gives hope for rest from all that burdens us and more.

1. Genesis 2:2–3. When God finished His creative work, He rested. God was not tired. He stopped to contemplate and enjoy all He had made. God wants us to stop our work and rest on the seventh day as well. Why do you think this is necessary?

2. Genesis 18:2–5. Abraham saw three men at his door. He offered water to wash their feet and fresh bread to eat. He wanted to refresh them. Why do people need refreshing and rest?

3. Exodus 23:10–12. The Sabbath laws required six days of work and a day of rest—for man, his servants, and his animals. Even the land was to lie dormant in the seventh year. Why do some

think no special rest is needed on the seventh day, or at least one day of the week? Do you think we pay for this lack of rest?

4. 2 Chronicles 14:1–6. King Asa of Judah tore down idols and led his people to honor God. No wars broke out during his rule. Would such a thing happen in our day? Why not?

5. Psalm 55:6–8. How does the psalmist describe rest? What burdens in your life make you want to fly away? Do we need to escape, or can we find rest in the midst of activity?

6. Psalm 132:14–15. God chose Zion as His dwelling place. How does God find in His people a resting place? Does God provide for His own?

7. Isaiah 28:12. God offered a resting place for His people. They did not listen to God. They became ensnared by their enemies. What happens to us when we disobey God?

8. Jeremiah 6:16. What ancient paths did God want His people to follow? What was their former way of life? What blessings come to those who live God's way?

9. Matthew 11:28–29. What invitation does Christ give to those who are weary? Why do we get worn out sometimes? How do we find rest for our souls?

10. Hebrews 4:3, 9–11. Since we believe in the Lord, what should be our heritage and blessing now? How can we enter God's rest (not only in heaven but also here on earth)?

Rewards

76

Abraham Lincoln borrowed a book on the life of George Washington from a neighbor. One rainy night he sat up late reading the book and put it down in what he thought was a safe place in the family's log cabin. The next morning Lincoln found the book soaking wet. He took it back to the neighbor farmer and offered to work in the man's cornfield for three days to pay for the book because he didn't have any money. When the work in the field was done, the man gave Lincoln the book as a reward for his work. Almost everyone appreciates rewards, and the Bible is not silent on the topic. Encouraging words are given to everyone who serves God and others with love and faithfulness.

1. Genesis 15:1, 7. When Abraham left his home near Babylon, what became his reward? What additional promise did the Lord make to Abraham? How did he gain righteousness? How can our earthly pilgrimage bring rewards?

2. Ruth 2:1–12. Who was Ruth? What did she do that impressed Boaz? How did Boaz reward her? Did God also reward her? Read the rest of the story.

3. 1 Samuel 30:20–24. Enemies had plundered many of the possessions of David's army. Some of his men recovered the goods

while others stayed by the stuff. What reward did those who stayed behind receive? What's the application?

4. 2 Chronicles 15:5–9. What was good King Asa told to do? How did he show that he had courage? How did the Lord reward him? Does God reward us for our work done in obedience to Him?

5. Psalms 19:8–11. How does God reward those who keep His commands? In reading this passage, do you see the intrinsic reward in walking in the beauty of His ways? Do you anticipate a great reward?

6. Proverbs 11:18. If we want a sure reward, what must we do? How can we sow righteousness? What kind of wages do the wicked earn? What kind of sower are you?

7. Proverbs 25:21–22. How do some nations treat their enemies? How do we treat individuals who offend us? Kindness has a way of convicting and subduing an enemy. And God rewards kindness! What would happen in our world if everyone practiced this principle of kindness?

8. Matthew 5:10–12. Have you ever been persecuted and hated because of your faith? This is common in many countries of the world. What reward awaits the persecuted? When?

9. Matthew 10:40–42. What kind of reward is given those who receive a prophet or other servant of God? This is incredible to contemplate. Discuss the possibilities. Are ordinary acts of kindness toward those with ordinary needs also rewarded? God seems to be in the business of rewards!

10. 1 Corinthians 3:8–14. What is the basis of rewards? If a believer's life is genuine and his work honest, he will receive a reward. What happens to the one who builds carelessly?

Riches

77

Who are some of the wealthiest people in the world today? The Bible states that the silver and gold and the cattle on a thousand hills are in God's portfolio. The Lord of the universe lets man have possession of certain things for a while, but eventually everything falls back into God's corner. When we talk about riches, we can't say that wealth is good or evil within itself. The way we handle riches determines its status. Many rich people are righteous and many poor people are evil. The reverse is also true. Look at some examples of wealthy people in the Scriptures:

1. Genesis 13:1–2. When God called Abraham from Babylon, he was wealthy. What did he own? Can people of wealth be godly and righteous?

2. Psalm 62:10. Is it easy or hard to gain wealth? Is there more than one way to gain it? If a person becomes rich honestly, what care should be taken? What are some difficulties with the handling of wealth?

3. Proverbs 10:4. What kind of disposition must a person have who wants to gain wealth? What do those who refuse to work accumulate?

4. Proverbs 18:11. Can wealth be like a strong tower or a fortified city? Why or why not? Can there be a false security connected with plenty? Who or what is our hope?

5. Proverbs 27:23–24. Is there a certain diligence to keeping one's wealth? What can cause the collapse of riches? Is wealth a perpetual entity? What does Proverbs 23:4 teach about gaining wealth?

6. Jeremiah 9:23–24. What temptation does a person with wealth face? What should be the object of a believer's "boasting"?

7. Matthew 19:23–26. Why did Jesus say it is hard for a rich person to enter heaven? What of Abraham, Job, and Barnabas? What things are made possible with God?

8. Matthew 27:57. Joseph of Arimathea witnessed the crucifixion of Christ. How did this wealthy man show his faith? Is there sometimes a divine purpose for wealth? How can we prove our faith in poverty or in plenty?

9. 2 Corinthians 8:9. What was the status of Jesus before He came to this world? Why did He become poor? How has Christ made us rich? (See 1 Corinthians 3:21–23.) Are there other ways to be rich besides material wealth?

10. Revelation 2:9. What commendation did the church at Smyrna receive from Jesus? How was that poor church also rich? How can any church or person be rich?

78

Saints

Through the centuries, God's people have been known by various names. The Old Testament covenant people were called Hebrews, Israelites, or Jews. Today we call a person who believes in Jesus a Christian. Sometimes we mention a particular church or denomination in order to identify someone as a Christian (e.g., Baptist, Methodist, Presbyterian). One prominent name in both the Old and New Testaments to identify God's people is *saint*. This name means a believer who has been redeemed by God's grace. The Scriptures and personal experience indicate that there are exemplary saints in the world, but there are also those who may bring reproach to God's cause. The Bible mentions saints more than one hundred times. It has been said, "To live with saints in heaven will be bliss and glory, but to live with saints upon the earth—well, that's another story!" Let's review a few of the references to saints found in the Bible.

1. Deuteronomy 33:2–4. God had many saints around Him at Sinai. What do the words mean that the saints are in God's hand and sit at His feet? What about us?

2. Psalm 30:4. When will you begin the habit of "singing to the Lord"? It is perhaps one of the most common forms of praise

for God's holiness and giving Him thanks for all He has done for us. Talk about other forms of praise.

3. Psalm 37:28–29. What does it mean that God does not forsake His saints and preserves them forever? What do you think about our being eternally secure in God's keeping? Discuss the different views of this doctrine.

4. Psalm 116:15. How does the word *precious* as applied to the death of His saints encourage you? Why does God look upon a believer or saint's death as a special or priceless event?

5. Matthew 27:52. What happened in a cemetery in Jerusalem when Christ died? After His resurrection, what did some of the previously dead do? Discuss your ideas.

6. Acts 26:10–11. What did Paul say he had done to the saints in Jerusalem and in other places? Who were those saints? Where and how are saints persecuted today?

7. Romans 15:25–26. Do some of God's saints live with abundance? How can some saints help the destitute? What are we doing for third-world saints or Christians?

8. 1 Corinthians 6:2–3. Do you have any idea how saints will judge the world in the future? Had you ever thought that we would also judge angels? Discuss this.

9. 1 Thessalonians 3:12–13. What can be done to establish the saints in holiness before God? Who will be with Christ when He comes again?

10. Jude 1:3–4. Who are the saints Jude wrote to? How has the faith been delivered to the saints? What does Jude warn them about?

Salvation

79

When a serious accident happens on a highway, we may say that the "jaws of life" saved the victims. When someone is pulled from a burning building, some will say the fire fighters saved the person. Sometimes the Old Testament refers to salvation as God's spiritual rescue of His people, but at other times it is a way of expressing God's deliverance from some physical danger, such as what Jonah faced (2:7–10). The word *salvation* appears in the Old Testament about one hundred twenty times. The New Testament uses the word about forty times, and most of those references point to salvation in the spiritual sense. For example, 2 Timothy 1:9 tells us, "[God] has saved us and called us to a holy life" (NIV). Salvation not only saves us from sin but also gives us a personal relationship with Jesus Christ. God in His fullness is involved in our salvation.

1. Exodus 14:13. When Moses prepared to lead the Israelites out of Egypt, God told the nation to stand still and see His salvation. What did he mean when he said the Egyptians they saw that day they would never see again? Do you think Moses understood the real meaning of what he was saying? Read the rest of the story in this chapter of Exodus.

2. Psalm 27:1–3. The Psalms mention God's salvation more than

any other book. How did David describe God and His salvation? How could he have such confidence in the face of his enemies?

3. Isaiah 12:2–3. Isaiah emphasizes God himself as his salvation. What other blessings does he mention? What attitude accompanies taking in the fruits of salvation?

4. Matthew 1:21–23. Who did God choose to fulfill the prophecy of the coming Messiah? Should Mary be called the Mother of God? Why not? What does *Immanuel* mean?

5. Matthew 8:23–27. Why were the disciples afraid? Do physical dangers disturb you? Some concern is normal; constant worry and fretting is not. How concerned is Jesus for our physical as well as spiritual salvation? Who is in control of your life?

6. Luke 2:25–32. What did the Holy Spirit reveal to Simeon? Who did Simeon see in God's temple in Jerusalem? What great promise did God give through Jesus?

7. Acts 4:12. What does this verse state about salvation? How many paths lead to heaven? Does "no other name under heaven" sound exclusive? Why or why not? Is there another way to get to heaven besides through Jesus?

8. Acts 16:20–34. Why were Paul and Silas in prison? What happened to them first? Why was the jailer frightened? What message did he hear? What action showed that he believed?

9. Romans 10:9–10. Explain what "confessing Jesus as Lord" means. What is essential to salvation? How is salvation received?

10. Ephesians 2:8–10. Explain the meaning of God's grace. What are the requirements for being saved? If works don't save us, what is their purpose? (James 2:14–22).

Sanctification 80

In chapter 8 of Leviticus, God told Moses to wash Aaron and his sons with water so they would be clean. Then Aaron and his sons were clothed with priestly garments. After those ceremonial steps, Moses anointed them and the tabernacle and its furnishings with oil to indicate that they were set apart or sanctified for God's holy purposes.

Sanctification is a word that reminds us that God is set apart from everything that is unholy. Sanctification in relation to God's people is a permanent spiritual position (we are forever and fully set apart); but on the other hand, sanctification is a process whereby God continues to produce Christlikeness in the life of a believer. We stand on holy ground as we consider the holiness doctrine of consecration, or sanctification.

1. Genesis 2:3. After six days of creating, how did God set apart the seventh day? What commandment requires the same of God's people? How should God's people sanctify every day?

2. Joshua 3:5. What was the prerequisite for God doing amazing things among His people? Have you been sanctified, set apart, and consecrated to the Lord?

3. 2 Chronicles 31:11–12, 18, 20–21. What orders did Hezekiah give concerning storerooms? How and why were the genealogical

records established? How did Hezekiah show his faithfulness and consecration to God?

4. John 17:17–18. What did Christ ask His Father to do for His people? For what purpose are we set apart? How do we follow in Christ's footsteps?

5. 1 Corinthians 1:2. Paul is addressing the church of God in Corinth, a people called to be holy, sanctified. But the letter mentions some shocking revelations (3:1; 5:1). How are the believers described in 3:1? What sin is discovered in 5:1 that is rarely found even among pagans?

6. Colossians 2:14–16. (See also Luke 10:8; Acts 11:5–9; 1 Corinthians 10:27; 1 Timothy 4:3–5.) What did Jesus nail to the cross? How does this fact give us grounds for disregarding others' judgments against us? How can food be sanctified? How do these words release us today to have a freer outlook on the foods we eat and the days we observe or don't observe?

7. 1 Thessalonians 4:3–7. What is God's will for us? What should a sanctified person avoid? How is sanctification a realized state and also a process?

8. 1 Thessalonians 5:23. Can you explain what it means for God to sanctify you through and through? Does this mean sinless perfection? What does it mean to be blameless at the coming of the Lord?

9. Hebrews 13:12–13. What does it mean that "Jesus suffered outside the city gate"? (NIV). How does Christ make us holy through His blood? How do we bear the disgrace He bore?

10. 1 Peter 1:1–2. Who are God's elect, or chosen, people? Does God's foreknowledge affect our choice? What person of the Godhead sanctifies us? How does sanctification affect our obedience?

Satan—
the Devil

81

Bank robbers and other crooks who want to deceive people often have an alias or an assumed name. They do most of their work by being deceptive. Satan, who works by deception also, has various names, such as the Dragon, the Serpent, the Devil, and the Father of Lies. Satan is the world's mastermind counterfeiter or pretender. Look at a few of the actions of the one who once was the chief of God's angels:

1. Genesis 3:1–15. How did the devil become involved in man's sin? Who did Adam blame for his sin? Who did Eve blame? (Does this sound familiar?) What did God tell the devil about his future? Why and in what ways is the devil busy in today's world?

2. Job 1:6–12, 21. Why did God allow such severe testing of Job? Why does Satan attack God's character? (both in this narrative and in the Genesis 3 passage above). In what ways does the Evil One attack people today?

3. Zechariah 3:1–5. What had Satan done to Joshua, God's high priest? (Not Joshua who worked with Moses.) What does Satan do today?

4. Luke 22:31–34. Why did Jesus warn Peter of Satan's attacks? Did Peter succumb to temptation? What is our escape when Satan tempts us?

5. John 8:42–44. How did Jesus describe Satan in this text? Do you think our enemy ever gives up on us? If a person does not belong to Jesus, who is in control of his life?

6. 1 Corinthians 5:5. Why do you think Paul told the church in Corinth to commit a blatant sinner to the devil? What good could come of this action? Is this frightening? Discuss the possible reasons and outcomes.

7. 2 Corinthians 4:3–4. What is Satan called in this verse? What is the nature of his work? Why do you think the devil is seemingly successful in his worldwide work?

8. 1 Peter 5:8–9. How does Satan act like a lion? Does the devil disguise himself in other ways? What are we told to do in response to the devil's tactics?

9. 1 John 3:8–10. What is one reason Jesus came to this world? How are God's children and the devil's followers distinguished? Can we always identify each?

10. Revelation 20:1–3, 10. What is the final destiny of the devil? Do you think the Bible tells us enough about Satan? Why or why not? Is it possible to be too taken up with what he is doing? Give examples.

Senior Citizens— the Golden Years

82

Anyone who loves genealogy could have a field day with Genesis 5. It lists the prominent men who lived from Adam to Noah, telling us their ancestry and how old they were when they died. The oldest one in the list is Methuselah, who lived 969 years. Enoch was 365 years of age when God took him home. We would have no trouble calling the people in those centuries old, elderly, or senior citizens!

Robert Browning (1812–1889) wrote a poem entitled *Rabbi Ben Ezra*. The first few lines of the long poem include the following: "Grow old along with me. The best is yet to be; the last of life, for which the first was made." No one is going to eclipse Methuselah's long life. However, with the help of medical science and good health habits, many people reach the "golden years." Consider a few elderly people in the Bible from whom we may learn some good lessons:

1. Genesis 5:3–5. How old was Adam when his third son was born? What was his name? How old was Adam when he died? What about other children of Adam and Eve? (Genesis 4:1).

2. Genesis 23:1–9. What miracle happened in Sarah's life when she was old? (Genesis 21:2–3). How did Sarah set an example for women? How did Abraham show his love for Sarah when she died?

3. Deuteronomy 34:1–12. Where was Moses when he saw the Promised Land? What was Moses' age when he died and what was remarkable about him? Who buried him?

4. Joshua 14:6–13. What work did Caleb do when he was forty years old? What was his request as a senior citizen? In what ways is Caleb a role model for us?

5. Joshua 24:15, 23–32. What kind of family man was Joshua? What challenge and warning did he give to the Israelites? How can we follow Joshua's example?

6. 1 Samuel 2:11–12; 3:13; 4:10–18. Who was Eli and how did he fail God and his family? What happened during Israel's war? How old was Eli and how did he die?

7. Luke 2:25–35. Describe Simeon. What had the Holy Spirit revealed to him? What once-in-a-lifetime experience did he have? What did Simeon pray as he held Jesus in his arms? What did he say to Mary?

8. Luke 2:36–38. What spiritual disciplines did the prophetess Anna practice? Who did she meet in the temple? How old was she when she died?

9. John 21:18–19. What did Jesus tell Peter would happen to him when he was old? What does "stretch out your hands" mean in this passage? How may we glorify God in death as well as in life?

10. 2 Timothy 1:5; 3:15. Who was Timothy's grandmother and mother, and what kind of women were they? How important is it to teach our children the Scriptures from a young age? Is there a tendency to leave Christian teaching to the church?

Shepherds and Sheep

83

Goat and sheep ranches are common in many countries of the world. We hear about sheep, but not very much about shepherds. The Bible, however, is a sourcebook for this profession. We can learn about ourselves and also about Jesus as we look at references to shepherds and sheep in a spiritual context.

1. 1 Samuel 17:34–36. What did David tell Saul about his defending his father's sheep from wild animals? How did he compare this action to standing up against Goliath the Philistine?

2. Psalm 23:1–6. Who is our true shepherd? In what ways does He care for us? Will we lack for anything we need if we follow Him? How does the Lord deliver us from fear?

3. Isaiah 40:11. How does God take care of His flock? How does this text show His tenderness and compassion? Does He have special empathy for those with young children?

4. Ezekiel 34:1–6. What did many of Israel's so-called spiritual shepherds do rather than care for their people? What should be a shepherd's primary concern?

5. Luke 2:8–10. On the night when Christ was born in Bethlehem, to whom did an angel appear? Why were they initially afraid? Why do you think God thought it a good idea to tell poor shepherds the good news?

6. Luke 15:4–6. How valuable is one lost sheep to a shepherd? What does the story tell us about a shepherd's attitude toward his flock? How does this compare to a spiritual shepherd and flock, to Jesus and His children?

7. John 10:14–16. Why is Jesus called the Good Shepherd? Do His sheep know Him? Does He know them? How does He compare this relationship to that of His Father and Him?

8. John 21:15–17. How does Jesus reinstate Peter after his denial of Jesus? What seems to be the primary proof of love? What is required in any close relationship besides a declaration of love and commitment? How do we care for God's people?

9. 1 Peter 2:24–25. In what state were we when Christ died for us? Why do some of God's people continue to wander away from Him? What new name for Jesus is given in this text? Share experiences of wandering and being drawn back by the Shepherd.

10. 1 Peter 5:1–4. How might pastors serve God's people more effectively? What is the reward for good earthly shepherds of God's flock? Why is "lording it over" someone never productive?

Sin 84

People testing their shooting skills erect a target and try to hit the bull's-eye. In the spiritual life, when a person sins, it means he or she has missed the mark. *Sin* in Greek is *ha-mar-tia*. The Bible uses the word many times to indicate a failure to keep the law. Other words, such as *transgression, fault, iniquity,* and *disobedience* also indicate falling short of God's standard. Let's view sin in ten settings from the Bible.

1. Numbers 32:20–23. What stirred the Lord's anger? What was this tribe's responsibility before the Lord? What happens if we shirk our responsibilities?

2. Psalm 51:1–14. How does David show his remorse and shame before God for his sin? What results does David look for with the cleansing of his sin?

3. Proverbs 21:4. Why do you think "haughty eyes and a proud heart" are called "the lamp of the wicked"? (NIV). Are outward looks sometimes an indicator of inward corruption? Can we always judge by appearances?

4. Ecclesiastes 9:18. What is better than weapons of war? What is

the effect of one person who lives in sin? Contrast this with the effect of one person who lives for God.

5. Isaiah 1:18. What is the effect of the cleansing blood of Christ on sin? Can anyone provide a better remedy? What does this text show someone who sees sin as a stain that can never be removed?

6. Jeremiah 17:9; 13:23. How is the human heart described? Are we born with a sinful nature? Why can't personal goodness save us?

7. Matthew 27:3–4. What often happens after a person commits a glaring sin? What did Judas do about his remorse? Do a sinner's companions always sympathize with his regret?

8. John 8:3–11. What did the Pharisees do with the woman caught in adultery? What was Jesus' response? What did He say to the woman? Discuss why Jesus treated the situation the way He did.

9. Romans 3:23; 6:23. Is everyone guilty of sin? What is the cost of sin? What does God offer?

10. 1 Corinthians 8:1–13. Some things may not be wrong for us, but are wrong for someone else (with regard to behaviors that do not have moral quality). How can we sometimes exercise a freedom that becomes a stumbling block for a weak or immature Christian? Why is it important to nurture someone who is weak?

Sleep

85

Washington Irving (1783–1859), a famous American writer, is unknown to many today. In his *Sketch Book*, he created the story of Rip Van Winkle. Rip was a good-natured man who was too lazy to fish even when fish were biting, and he never complained about being henpecked and penniless. One day he wandered off into the Catskill Mountains of New York and met a group of dwarfs. One of the dwarfs gave Rip some liquor, and after drinking it, he fell into a twenty-year deep sleep. When he awoke as an old man with a long white beard, he returned home to find that his wife had died, his children had grown up, and the nation had elected George Washington as president. The Bible gives many examples of those who sleep. Consider the following references:

1. Genesis 2:21–23. Why did God cause Adam to fall into a deep sleep? What do you think was Adam's reaction when he awoke? Have you had unusual experiences with sleep—dreams, sleepwalking?

2. Genesis 28:10–16. When Jacob left home, do you think he felt uncomfortable that first night? What happened while he slept? Can God use dreams to speak to us while we sleep?

3. Psalm 121:1–8. Who constantly watches over us? Who is always

awake while we sleep? Do you ever thank God that He is constantly looking out for your well-being?

4. Psalm 127:2. Are you surprised that God gives sleep to those He loves? Do we sometimes think of Him as a taskmaster who requires constant diligence on our part? Next time you are awake at night remember this verse.

5. Proverbs 6:4–11. Solomon seems to be speaking to those who are lazy or sleep too much. What small insect teaches us about diligence and industry? What danger befalls a sluggard?

6. Matthew 13:25. What happens to those who sleep when they should be awake? Who is an enemy that can cause damage while His servants sleep? How?

7. Luke 9:30–32. What did Peter and his companions almost miss because they were dozing? What do we sometimes miss because of our lethargy? How and when do we face that risk?

8. Acts 12:6. What was Simon Peter doing in Jerusalem fastened between two guards? How could he sleep in this situation? What was the church doing to show their support?

9. Acts 20:7–12. Have you been in a worship service that was too long? What happened to Eutychus while Paul preached? How was Paul able to raise the man to life? What might have been the purpose of this incident?

10. Ephesians 5:14. Paul wrote about being asleep spiritually. Why do some Christians sleep and miss opportunities for service? What can Christ do for sleeping saints?

Spiritual Renewal—Revival

86

In his book *A Tale of Two Cities*, Charles Dickens (1812–1870) began with the words "It was the best of times, it was the worst of times; it was the age of wisdom, it was the age of foolishness. . . ." These words still speak to us.

Why does every generation know these contrasts? Is it always a bad sign? Is there a single solution to the problems of our day? A lot of people have ideas about this. But history testifies to the truth that real hope for the world comes through moral and spiritual renewal. The changes we need come alive when people get right with God and with one another. Many of the programs that man designs apart from God aggravate problems rather than alleviate them. The call for spiritual and religious revival needs to be shared in the marketplace if we expect society's needs to be met. Explore some Scriptures that talk about spiritual renewal.

1. Genesis 45:25–28; 48:2. What brought renewal and joy to Jacob? How can we bring joy and encouragement to family members and friends?

2. 2 Kings 13:20–21. What happened to the man who was buried

near Elisha's grave? What does this say about spiritual life that survives the grave?

3. Psalm 51:10–13. This should encourage every believer to ask God to renew a right spirit within him. What can happen to ministry if spiritual joy is restored?

4. Psalm 85:4–6. (See also 2 Chronicles 7:14.) What will take place when God restores and renews His people? What are the conditions for this to happen? Are we thirsty for an awakening?

5. Jeremiah 30:17–19. How do the promises God gave to Israel about their restoration apply to us? How should we respond to God's renewal of His people?

6. Hosea 6:1–3. When we return to the Lord, what does He promise to do? Talk about the paradox that God injures His people and then heals them. What miracles of nature remind us of God's renewal?

7. Romans 7:8–10. What does the law produce? How is sin revived? What should be our response?

8. Romans 12:2. Why do we need to experience a renewal of the mind? What discovery will spiritual renewal lead to?

9. 2 Corinthians 4:16–17. Why should believers not lose heart, even when their physical bodies suffer setbacks? What do our momentary troubles achieve for us?

10. Colossians 3:10–11. How does God renew us to His own image? What do we need to set aside? In Christ, we are one with other Christians regardless of cultural backgrounds or positions. When we realize this and embrace it, what are we experiencing?

Suffering and Pain

87

One unforgettable man in the Old Testament is Job. He lost his family, all his possessions, and finally his health. Do good people suffer? If we're completely committed to Christ, will a spiritual life and godly conduct assure us health and prosperity? Let's see what the Scriptures teach on the subject.

1. Jeremiah 20:1–2. Why was Jeremiah persecuted? Why do God's people still face dangers around the world?

2. Matthew 16:21. What did Jesus tell His disciples He must suffer? If the world treated Jesus this way, how can we expect any less?

3. Mark 8:31–33. Again, when Jesus mentioned the sufferings He would face, what did Peter do? What did Jesus say to him? Why is it hard to understand the things of God when we still have the mind of an earthling?

4. Acts 5:40–41. When the apostles suffered beatings and imprisonment soon after Pentecost, what did they do? Why was it hard to stop them from preaching about Jesus? How would you have reacted in the same situation?

5. Acts 9:16. When the Lord saved Paul on the road to Damascus, Paul heard something of the suffering he would face. What happened when Paul was filled with the Holy Spirit? Are we inoculated against difficult days?

6. Romans 8:17–18. The future of God's people is one of glory. And what does the Bible tell us is ours as followers of Jesus even before we reach glory? Is any suffering we may endure worth it?

7. 2 Corinthians 12:7–10. Why did Paul have to suffer what he called a "thorn in my flesh"? What did he pray? What promise did he receive? What was Paul's attitude toward suffering?

8. Philippians 1:29–30. God grants us the privilege of believing on Christ, but what sometimes accompanies our belief? For whom and for what cause do Christians suffer?

9. Hebrews 5:7–8. What kind of prayers did the Son of God offer? Why were His prayers heard? What did He learn from His sufferings? What can we learn from suffering for Christ?

10. Revelation 2:10. The church at Smyrna faced suffering. Who is said to have caused their suffering? What is the reward for faithfulness while suffering for Christ?

Tears—
Crying

Daniel Webster, orator and statesman, had a beautiful daughter named Grace. While still a baby, she became ill and died in his arms. It is said that Daniel Webster wept uncontrollably as he turned and walked away from his child's lifeless body.

Everyone cries at one time or another. Even a wedding may bring a joyful flood of tears to the bride or the groom and/or their parents. When death occurs, friends and family of the deceased suffer tears of sorrow, loss, and remembrance. When a person receives a reward for an outstanding work, tears of relief and joy may flow. When a sports team wins a big game, fans jump up and down in celebration, and even some tears may be shed. People of every race and age bracket cry. Allow these Scriptures that relate to tears speak to you:

1. Genesis 21:12–19. Who was Hagar? What did Abraham do with her and Ishmael? What was God's promise to Abraham concerning Hagar's offspring? Why was Hagar distraught? How did God answer her prayer?

2. 2 Kings 20:1–5. When Hezekiah was told he would die, what did he do? What was his plea before the Lord? What word from the Lord did Isaiah give him?

3. Esther 7:1–6; 8:1–3. What evil plans did Haman have? Who was Esther and what did she do about it? What did her action reveal about her heritage? How did her husband, the king, respond? What is the eventual fate of evildoers?

4. Psalm 6:1–6. To whom does David pour out his anguish? Have you ever felt like you could soak your couch with tears? What are some of the situations that bring on emotional distress and tears? How might we help those who are going through hard times?

5. Jeremiah 9:1. (See also Lamentations 2:18–19.) What was the cause of Jeremiah's grief? In whose presence should we pour out our hearts? How can we minister to those who mourn the loss of a loved one?

6. Luke 7:36–39, 44. Describe the scene in Simon the Pharisee's house. What did the woman do for Jesus? What was the Pharisee's response? How did Jesus rebuke Simon and credit the woman?

7. Acts 20:19, 31. Why did Paul say he served the Lord with many tears? What was his experience in Ephesus? What does Paul's example teach us about ministry?

8. Hebrews 5:7. Even the Son of Man knew strong crying and tears. (See also Matthew 23:37; 26:38–39; 27:46.) What else did He know as part of His human experience on earth?

9. Hebrews 12:16–17. (See also Genesis 25:25; 27:25–30.) Jacob and Esau were the twin sons of Isaac and Rebekah. What happened to cause Esau to shed tears of regret? Can tears come too late?

10. Revelation 21:4. What glorious thing will God do for His people in heaven? Why will there be no reason for tears in heaven? Comfort one another with this prospect.

Temptation

Martin Luther said, "You can't keep the birds from flying over your head, but you can keep them from building nests in your hair." Temptations fly all around us. However, we do not have to yield to them. John Bunyan, who wrote *The Pilgrim's Progress*, said that for an entire year he faced the temptation to sell Christ or deny Him. He said he could not eat, cut wood, or reach out to pick up something without the temptation flashing through his mind: "Sell Christ for this, sell Him for that! Sell Him! Sell Him!" He said he just could not get rid of the temptation to deny Christ for one day, one month, or one year, whatever he did. If any of you think you are the only person in the world hounded by temptation, take another look. Let's review some Scriptures that relate to temptation.

1. Genesis 39:7–9. What temptation did Joseph face? How did he escape it? Why did Joseph say such a sin would be against God?

2. Matthew 4:1–11. What do you think about the Spirit leading Jesus into the wilderness to be tempted? What three temptations did Jesus face? How did Jesus withstand them? How can we learn from Jesus' example here?

3. Matthew 6:13. What does Jesus mean in the words of the Lord's Prayer: "Lead us not into temptation"? Does God tempt His people? Who are we to be delivered from?

4. Mark 14:38. When Jesus prayed in Gethsemane, what were the disciples doing? What temptation was Jesus referring to? What is one way to avoid temptation?

5. 1 Corinthians 10:13. Why do you think temptations are common experiences of everyone? In what areas do temptations strike you? What is the promise to the tempted?

6. Galatians 6:1. How do you feel about anyone who falls victim to temptation, whether it is theft, profanity, angry outbursts, or something else? Should the fallen be rejected?

7. 1 Thessalonians 3:5. What was Paul's concern? Why does the devil seem to look upon God's people as a prize to be won? Because Satan sometimes wins the victory, should that stop us from our work to teach and nurture others?

8. Hebrews 2:17–18. What was the reason for Jesus' temptations? In what ways is He like us? How can He help those who are tempted?

9. Hebrews 4:15–16. Since Jesus endured temptation without falling, how does He feel about those of us who are tempted, even if we succumb to temptation? What resource is ours through Him?

10. James 1:13–14. What does James say about a believer who is tempted? What are some causes of temptation? What does James 4:7 say about victory over them?

Time

Harvard University's founding fathers placed a sundial on campus with the following inscription: "Upon every minute hangs eternity." Read those words again. Those early spiritual leaders wanted every student to understand the value of time. Earthly life involves time—minutes, hours, days, months, and years—1,440 minutes in each day and about 518,000 minutes in a year. A person forty years of age has lived a little more than 20 million minutes. Time waits for no one. The Bible mentions *time* again and again, challenging all of us to recognize the importance of every moment. Let's make some life-changing discoveries that relate to time.

1. Numbers 20:15–16. Moses reminded the Hebrews that they had lived in Egypt a long time. Why do we sometimes stay in "Egypt" and not where we belong? Should we be moving on, or have we moved on?

2. 1 Chronicles 12:31–32. Israel's tribe of Issachar understood their times and wanted David to be king. What kind of times are we living in? Though we show respect to those in authority over us and our land, who is our King?

3. Psalm 41:1. In times of trouble, God delivers those who help

the weak or less fortunate. Do we face any kind of trouble? Who will deliver us?

4. Psalm 56:3. How can we trust the Lord during uncertain times? When dangerous times come, how do we respond? Why are many fearful today?

5. Psalm 119:126. When is it time for God to act, according to the psalmist? What is God's response when people disregard His Word? Does He always judge sin immediately? What do many people think of God and the Scriptures in our time?

6. Ecclesiastes 3:1–8. Is it comforting to know there is a time for everything? Discuss in your group the advantage of there being a right time for the occasions listed in these verses.

7. Acts 3:19–20. What do you think Simon Peter meant by "times of refreshing"? Why do we need times like that? What is needed for us to have a spiritual awakening?

8. Ephesians 5:15–16. How can we make the most of every opportunity given us? How do some of us waste time? Why should we be redeeming the time? How can we make better use of our time?

9. Hebrews 5:12. What do some of us need before we can become teachers of others? Why do some still need others to teach them the basics of the Christian faith even though they have been in the church for years?

10. 1 Peter 1:17. If we understand that God will judge us according to our use of time, how should we spend it? Why are we called sojourners or strangers here on earth?

Tithes and Offerings

91

Years ago, Dr. George W. Truett, of the First Baptist Church of Dallas, spoke about stewardship at a cowboy camp meeting near Fort Stockton, Texas. A rancher invited Truett to go with him for a ride across his ranch. The rancher said, "Dr. Truett, look to the north, east, south, and west. All that you see is mine. At least I thought so until today. Now I know it all belongs to God. Pray that I will surrender all that I own to the Lord." The pastor prayed and then the rancher prayed and dedicated himself and his ranch to the Lord. At that very hour, the rancher's son, who was living in rebellion, felt moved by the Spirit of God and surrendered his life to the Lord. He came to the evening service, made a profession of faith, and said that he wanted to live for God. When we surrender self and substance to God, He will bless us. Here are some Scriptures about giving to God and His cause.

1. Exodus 35:22; 36:5; Deuteronomy 14:28–29. Is there a limit to what can be given to God's cause? Who is blessed by our gifts? What is God's response?

2. Deuteronomy 26:9–12. Why were the Israelites' firstfruits given to God? Who did their tithes support besides the Levites or religious leaders? Who else was helped by their gifts?

3. Proverbs 11:24–25. How can that which is given freely be increased? What happens to the one who withholds his wealth? What about the generous person? Who is blessed besides the one who receives our gifts? Do financial gifts guarantee financial prosperity?

4. Malachi 3:10. What is a tithe? How does our giving help God's work? What does God promise to those who "test" Him in this? What blessings fill your life?

5. Matthew 6:19–21. What caution does Jesus give about large bank accounts? How have financial losses come about today? Why is heaven the best place for treasures? Where is your heart?

6. Matthew 23:23. Pharisees in New Testament times thought that tithing would make them acceptable to God. When are gifts accepted and honored by God?

7. Luke 6:38. When a person gives or shares financially in God's work, does the giving deprive him or her? Why not? What other ways may we give and be blessed? Can we ever out-give God?

8. Luke 21:1–4. Jesus noticed as people put gifts in the temple treasury in Jerusalem. Whom did He commend? Why? Should we give all we own?

9. Acts 20:33–35. How did Paul support himself? (Acts 18:1–3). Did he accept money from his churches? How does his experience relate to bi-vocational work? What words from Jesus did Paul quote?

10. 2 Corinthians 9:6. Should a farmer plant more seed if he wants a larger harvest? How does this truth apply to giving? What should be our attitude toward giving?

Tongue— Tongues

92

The tongue has a language of its own, doesn't it? Adolf Hitler was extremely influential in Germany because of his "inflamed tongue." The tongue has also brought encouragement and hope to millions with words of comfort and challenge. The tongue is a powerful instrument for good or for evil. It is the one member of the body that does not have to be pushed to have all the exercise it needs. What did Paul write about a bugle (or trumpet) that gives an uncertain sound? (1 Corinthians 14:8). Look at these passages about the tongue:

1. Exodus 4:10. God spoke to Moses about becoming the leader of the Israelites, but Moses said he was not eloquent and had a stammering tongue. Have you ever told God something similar?

2. Psalm 71:24. What was David's goal for his tongue? What was David thankful for? What do you praise God for today, besides your salvation?

3. Psalm 137:6. What did David say would happen to his tongue if he forgot Jerusalem? If we have a tongue to speak, who deserves our praise?

4. Proverbs 21:23. What does it mean to keep or guard our tongue? How difficult is this to do? How can the control of the tongue keep a person out of trouble?

5. Isaiah 50:4. Why do you think God gave Isaiah an instructed tongue? What did Isaiah say he would do to help the weary? What advantage is there to listening to the Lord?

6. Isaiah 54:17. What evil weapons sometimes come against God's people? What power enables us to refute those who accuse us? Who is our vindicator?

7. Luke 16:24. In the parable of Lazarus and the rich man, what did the rich man ask Abraham to do for him? What lesson can be drawn from this story today?

8. Acts 2:5–11. During the Pentecost season, people came to Jerusalem from many nations. How were they able to hear the message of Jesus in their own language?

9. Acts 19:4–7. Paul laid hands on twelve disciples of John the Baptist. They were filled with the Holy Spirit. Those believers spoke in tongues and prophesied. What does it mean to speak in tongues? (1 Corinthians 12:4-10). (See also Acts 8:14–17.)

10. James 1:26. If a person says he is religious but does not keep a rein on his tongue, what two things are true in his life? Do you at times have trouble controlling your tongue? Explain.

Trials— 93
Tribulations

John Bunyan (1628–1688) faced a jail sentence of twelve years in Bedford, England, because he was not licensed and registered in the state church, and he preached to those who did not conform to the state church. His wife had died two years earlier. He had four children, and among them was a daughter who was born blind. The Bedford preacher-writer married again, and his second wife became pregnant. When Bunyan was sent to prison, his wife suffered premature labor. Many people face multiple trials.

One stanza of a hymn by Charles Albert Tindley has these words: "Trials dark on every hand, and we cannot understand all the ways that God would lead us to that blessed promised land; but He'll guide us with His eye, and we'll follow till we die, for we'll understand it better by and by." The Bible gives valuable insights on trials.

1. Matthew 13:20–21. In the parable of the sower some receive the Word with joy but then fall away when there are problems. Do you think these people were ever truly saved? (John 10:27–30). Discuss this in your group. Do some fall away and then return to the Lord?

2. Matthew 24:15-21. (See also Mark 13:14–20.) Many scholars believe Jesus is speaking of Rome's destruction of Jerusalem in

AD 70, stating that there would never be another tribulation of that magnitude. Or is He speaking of the great tribulation? (Revelation 7:9–14). Discuss this topic among yourselves.

3. John 16:33. What assurance did Jesus give the apostles? What should be our attitude toward trials we face today? What will we have as long as we are in this world?

4. Acts 14:19–22. Paul was stoned at Lystra. Did it deter him from preaching the gospel? What did he say about anyone entering God's kingdom? Where are some Christians facing trials today because of their faith?

5. 2 Corinthians 1:5–8. How does a Christian experience Christ's suffering? What are some positive results that come from trials and tribulations?

6. 2 Corinthians 6:4–10. Talk about Paul's long list of trials. How did he respond to mistreatment? Will Christians escape trials in this life? Why or why not?

7. Philippians 1:29–30. What two privileges do Christians share? Do you think Paul's struggles were related to his pushing back and continuing to do what he felt called to do? Will we suffer trials if we sit back and do nothing?

8. Hebrews 11:35–38. It is hard to imagine the agony that many Old Testament believers faced. Is it possible some in our day will also face such difficult times? Why or why not?

9. 1 Peter 4:12–13. Paul told the first-century Christians not to be surprised at the painful trials they faced. How would you react to such treatment? Is there a positive side to trials?

10. Revelation 7:14–17. These verses refer to those who are coming out of tribulation in the past as well as at the end times. What is the future hope of those who endure tribulation?

Trinity

How do we explain electricity? It is one of the many things we can't fully explain. In a similar way, God in His majesty and greatness remains somewhat of a mystery. God loves and blesses His people, but to explain God in all of His manifestations can never be done. However, we can trust Him. Man is limited and finite, but God is infinite. And yet God reveals himself as Father, Son, and Holy Spirit.

The Bible never uses the word *Trinity*. But the Trinitarian concept appears many times throughout the Bible so that we may understand God a little better. A few examples are Genesis 3:22; 11:7; and Isaiah 6:8. The *us* suggests a "tri-unity" or three in one—God the Father, Jesus the Son, and the Holy Spirit. Look at these Scriptures that indicate some of the ways in which God expresses himself:

1. Genesis 1:1–2, 26. God's name *Elohim* (Hebrew) is a plural noun that has a singular verb, as "the family is." Who is included in the Trinity? Notice that God says in verse 26: "Let *us* make man in *our* image. . . ."

2. Matthew 3:16–17. Who baptized Jesus? How were the Holy Spirit, Jesus, and the Father involved in the process? Do we see the triune God in that experience?

3. Matthew 28:18–20. How is the three-in-one God involved in this text? What mission did Jesus give His followers? What promise did Jesus give?

4. 1 Corinthians 12:3–6. What is a Christian able to say about Jesus by the Spirit of God? How is the Trinity involved in this confession?

5. 2 Corinthians 13:14. How does this benediction teach about the three-in-one God? What is the source of grace, love, and fellowship? Do these speak to different expressions of God?

6. Ephesians 1:11–14. The triune God brings about our salvation and eternal redemption. What part does the Son have? What is the contribution of the Holy Spirit? Whose possession are we?

7. Titus 3:4–7. What are we saved by if not by our righteous acts? What are we heirs of? Describe the works of the Father, Son, and Holy Spirit in this text.

8. Hebrews 9:14. How does the sacrifice of Christ differ from the sacrifice of goats and bulls and heifers? How may we serve the living God? Notice how each member of the Trinity has a part in our redemption.

9. 1 John 2:20–23. How do we know the truth? What do we call someone who denies that Jesus is the Christ? Since the Trinity consists of the Father, Son, and Holy Spirit, if we have the Son, who else do we have in our lives?

10. Jude 1:1–2, 20–21. Jude addresses his letter to those who are called and kept. Who calls us? Who keeps us? The three ministries of the Trinity are mentioned again in verse 2. How are we built up in our faith? What ministry of Christ gives us eternal life?

Vain or Vanity

95

The Pilgrim's Progress, the well-known Christian classic by John Bunyan, tells about Pilgrim, who travels from the City of Destruction to the Celestial City. On the way to heaven he passes through a town named Vanity, and in this town there is a place called Vanity Fair. Everything sold there appeals to a person's vanity: houses, lands, honors, pleasures, lusts, silver, gold, and the list goes on. At Vanity Fair everyone lives in sin and mocks or persecutes those who live a moral or ethical lifestyle. People like those of Vanity Fair populate our world today. The book of Ecclesiastes describes the life apart from God as one of vanity. Thirty verses state that everything is vanity unless it relates to God. We make choices: Life can be spent in empty, vain pursuits, or it can be full of purpose. Let's consider some Scriptures that give insights into the vain way of life.

1. Deuteronomy 32:40–47. To whom does vengeance belong? Men may vow to take care of themselves by the sword, but where does real life come from? What words are worth our time learning and observing? (See Deuteronomy 6:4–12.) What blessings come from following God's Word?

2. Job 7:3–4. Job said he endured months of vanity and futility.

What is he describing? When sleep doesn't come, what does man wait for? How can we better face work and weariness?

3. Psalm 2:1–4. What kind of vain plotting do people do? (Acts 4:24–27). Why is this vanity? What is God's response to those who rebel against Him and His Son?

4. Psalm 127:1–2. What happens to work we try to accomplish without God? Why is rising early and retiring late toiling for food in vain? What does God grant those He loves?

5. Proverbs 12:11. What does working the land produce? How is a vain person described? A good work ethic curbs vanity. Why is honest work honorable?

6. Malachi 3:13–15. Why do some think it is vain to serve God? Do their motives come into play? Why is it the correct choice to honor God's Word and live by it?

7. Romans 1:21–28. Why do you think the people described probably knew *of* God but didn't truly *know* Him? What happens when men and women give themselves over to the lusts of the flesh rather than honoring their bodies as God created them to be?

8. 1 Corinthians 15:14, 17. Why would preaching be in vain without the resurrection of Jesus? Why would faith be in vain if Christ had not been raised from the dead?

9. James 1:26. In what ways does religion become vain, empty, and useless? How does a person deceive himself?

10. 2 Peter 2:15–18. What is the future of proud, boastful people? What do such people want to do? What do evil people promise to others? What is their true condition?

Voices

96

Joan of Arc, French saint and national heroine (1412–1431), heard voices speaking to her during her teenage years. She was tried as a heretic and burned at the stake in Rouen, France, on May 30, 1431. When religious authorities asked why she did what she was doing, Joan of Arc told them voices spoke to her. When church leaders asked why they did not hear the voices, Joan told them that they were not listening.

We need to listen to God's voice. He speaks through creation, the Bible, through the lives of people, and by the Holy Spirit. We should be deaf to the voice of the world and the devil, but alert to God's voice. Let's go to the Scriptures for the topic of voices.

1. Exodus 5:1–2. When Moses and Aaron visited Pharaoh, what did they ask of him? How did Pharaoh respond? Why do people question God's voice?

2. 1 Kings 19:1–18. Why did Elijah go to Mount Horeb? What did God ask Elijah? What commission did he receive? Does God still have fresh orders for His people?

3. Job 4:12–19. In the midst of Job's suffering, describe what he saw. What two questions are asked? How do you think you would respond to the suffering Job endured?

4. Psalm 42:4. What kind of voice did David have as he went into God's house? What kind of attitude (voice) should we have both in the church and in the routines of everyday life?

5. Isaiah 6:1–4. What vision did Isaiah have when Israel's king died? What did that display signify? What did the angelic beings say? How is God's message conveyed to us today?

6. Isaiah 40:2–3. Whose voice would later be heard in the desert? (Matthew 3:3). What was the message in Isaiah and later in Matthew? What is our message today?

7. Jeremiah 3:11–15. What did the voice of God say to Israel? If they heard and repented, what blessing would they receive? What happens if we hear the Word of the Lord but don't heed it?

8. Ezekiel 33:30–32. What is said about Ezekiel's preaching and the people's response to it? Does it do any good to hear the words and not practice them? Is this a common response to God's message today? Why or why not?

9. Revelation 3:20. Who knocks at the door of every heart? Who must open the door? What happens when we let Him come in?

10. Revelation 11:15. What did the voices in heaven say when the seventh angel blew his trumpet? What will happen to the kingdoms of this world when Jesus returns to reign forever?

War— Warfare

97

Second Chronicles 13 tells about a war between the ten northern tribes of Israel and the two southern tribes of Judah. Jeroboam, son of Nebat, decided to attack the two southern tribes of Judah and Benjamin. King Abijah, of the two southern tribes, warned Jeroboam not to attack him and his army of 400,000. However, Jeroboam ordered his army of 800,000 to go to war against the two smaller tribes. When the northern forces attacked, Abijah called upon the Lord to save them. The Bible states that one half million soldiers of Jeroboam's army died in battle in one day. What an incredible slaughter!

The world has been plagued with wars since the beginning of time. When we read history books, we find that a great part of the events are related to war. The cost of war, both financially and in lives lost, should be a shock to everyone. There are also spiritual wars that go on within the souls of men. Let's look at the topic of war and warfare.

1. 1 Chronicles 5:18–22. A war began between the descendants of Hagar and Sarah. Why did God give the victory to His people? What did the Hagarites lose?

2. Ecclesiastes 9:17–18. Why are quiet words better heard than

shouts? What are some solutions, if any, to the problem of war? How do you interpret the second part of verse 18?

3. Isaiah 2:4; Micah 4:3. How would God intervene if we allowed Him to? What do these two prophets tell us about a warless world?

4. Isaiah 41:11–13. What happens to those who war against God's people? What does God promise? What is His counsel to His children?

5. Luke 14:31. What does a wise king do before he leads his forces into battle? What does this teach us about following Jesus into spiritual warfare?

6. Luke 21:5–9. Until Christ returns, what is going to continue in the world? Why will a big change not take place today? What is our hope in the midst of unrest?

7. 2 Corinthians 10:3–5. How is spiritual warfare different from the world's battles? What kinds of weapons do Christians have? How do we use our spiritual weapons?

8. James 4:1–2. What did James say causes quarrels among God's people? Why don't we get what we want? Can we pray in the wrong way?

9. Revelation 12:7–9; 19:19; 20:10. Who was cast out of heaven? What was the war in heaven about? What is Satan's final destiny?

10. Revelation 16:12–16. (See also 2 Thessalonians 2:8.) What is the last battle about? Who is Christ telling to be ready when He returns? Who will be revealed when Christ returns? What will happen to him?

Water   98

One of South America's most impressive sights is Iguazu Falls. These waterfalls, bordering Brazil, Paraguay, and Argentina, attract thousands of visitors every year and are truly impressive, but water in almost any form gets everyone's attention from the youngest child to the oldest adult. Almost all of us are drawn to the oceans, rivers, lakes, and waterfalls.

Without water, life as we know it would end, but water can also be dangerous. Much of our water is not potable, for instance. And we all recognize the blessing or blight that can come from rain-laden clouds. Samuel Taylor Coleridge painted a glowing word picture of water in *The Rime of the Ancient Mariner*. He wrote, "Water, water, everywhere, and all the boards did shrink; water, water, everywhere, nor any drop to drink." Let's look at a few lines about water from a biblical perspective.

1. Genesis 49:4. How was Jacob's son Reuben first described? But then he became turbulent, or unstable, as water, falling into serious sin. Why do some fall away like Reuben? How can someone become faithful, well-established, dependable?

2. Exodus 14:26. When God freed the Hebrews from Egypt, what

did Pharaoh's army do? What judgment befell them? How was Israel spared in the Red Sea?

3. 2 Kings 2:19–21. What did Elisha discover near Jericho? How did he restore the water? Whom did he credit with the miracle?

4. Psalm 42:1. How is spiritual thirst compared to the thirst of a deer? What does God provide to quench the thirst of His people?

5. Isaiah 44:1–4. What happens when water is poured on a dry, thirsty land? What is promised to Jacob in this passage? What must it be like to live near God's flowing streams?

6. Jeremiah 2:13. Describe a cistern. What about a broken one? When people forsake God, the Living Water, what do they have? Why do you think people sometimes settle for so much less than God offers?

7. John 7:37–39. What invitation does Jesus give to those who have spiritual thirst? To what is His Spirit compared? What happens to those who receive Jesus? What flows from a believer's life?

8. 1 Corinthians 3:6. We can all have a part in God's work. How can we water the places where God's work is happening? Who brings about the increase, or makes the "plants" grow? Can we take credit for the increase? Why or why not?

9. Revelation 22:1–2. What is the origin or source of the water of life? Why will it continue to flow? What does it nourish?

10. Revelation 22:17. Who gives the invitation for those who are thirsty? Why is the gift offered to everyone? Why is it free?

Wisdom

99

Socrates was born in Athens, Greece, about four hundred years before Christ. The world continues to talk and write about the wisdom of Socrates. Would you like to live and be remembered as a wise person? Solomon was probably the wisest man that ever lived and he wrote the book of Ecclesiastes. In chapter 12, verse 13, he gives us wisdom in a nutshell: "Fear God and keep his commandments" (NIV).

The Bible points out the path of wisdom for all who would follow it. Let's explore this topic, a source of pride to the ancient Grecians, and one of great interest to people in our day.

1. Job 28:28. According to Job, what is the source of wisdom? What does it mean to fear the Lord? Do most people have spiritual wisdom today? What is the advantage of shunning evil?

2. Psalm 104:24–25. When you contemplate the wonders of creation, how do you feel? What word is used in this text to indicate how God created all things?

3. Proverbs 4:7. What is our principal need in life? How do we get wisdom? How does wisdom demonstrate itself in life? What is it worth?

4. Matthew 13:54. When Jesus returned to Nazareth where He grew up, what did the people say of Him? Where did Christ get His wisdom and miraculous powers? Where do we get wisdom?

5. Luke 2:39–40. How is Jesus described at twelve years of age? What kinds of growth did Jesus experience? What else was evident in His life?

6. 1 Corinthians 3:18–20. How is the wisdom of this world described? Why does God look upon man's wisdom as vain?

7. Colossians 2:1–3. What three things did Paul desire for the church at Colosse? In whom are hidden all the treasures of wisdom and knowledge?

8. Colossians 4:5. What does Paul mean by saying we should be wise in the way we act toward outsiders, or non-Christians? Do you think we miss opportunities to witness because of our insensitivity to others?

9. James 1:5. Do you feel you lack wisdom? In what areas? If God is the source of wisdom, how do we get it? What is God's reaction when we make requests of Him?

10. James 3:17. Describe the wisdom that comes from heaven. Is God's wisdom demonstrated in our lives? Why or why not?

Wives— 100
Marriage

There are many good-natured jokes circulating about the creation of Eve. In one of them, Adam said to the Lord, "God, I love life in the garden, but I sometimes feel lonesome. Can you give me someone to be with me?" When the Lord asked man what he wanted, Adam began to describe his preferences. Then God said, "Adam, what you are asking might cost you an arm and a leg." Adam said, "Lord, what would you give me for a rib?"

Praise the Lord, He gave man a wife, the best earthly companion he could have. Someone once said that God made woman from the *side* of man so she could walk with him—not from his feet to trample upon him, or from his head to control his life. But again, from his side, in order to be his companion, counselor, and friend. Does anyone have the wisdom and authority to revamp God's design for the family? Let's look at some Scriptures about wives.

1. Genesis 2:18–25. Why did God give Adam a wife? What are some ways sin has distorted God's design for family life?

2. Genesis 3:1–20. How did the devil become involved in Eve's life? Why do you think he tempted Eve instead of Adam? What does Eve's name mean?

3. Genesis 24:1–4. Where did Abraham send his servant to get a wife for Isaac? Why didn't Isaac marry someone who lived nearby? Why is it important whom we choose to marry?

4. Job 2:9–10. What counsel did Job's wife give him? Why? What did Job say to her? What was Job not guilty of in this exchange? What do you think of Job's comment about what we accept from God?

5. Proverbs 18:22. Why is finding a wife a good thing? What blessings can come from God when a man marries? How can wives exemplify godliness in their marriage?

6. Ezekiel 24:14–18. How was Ezekiel judged? How did the Lord refer to Ezekiel's wife? Why was he not allowed to mourn her as was the custom? Was the incident a foretaste of loss among the people? Study the context of these verses.

7. Malachi 2:13–16. Why do you think marriages failed so often among the ancient Jews? How does God feel about divorce? How can God help when family life falls apart?

8. Matthew 22:23–30. What did the Sadducees ask Jesus? What did Jesus say about marriage in heaven? In what way will we be like the angels in heaven?

9. Titus 2:4–5. What is one of the roles of a wife in the church? What does it mean to be subject to your husband? Discuss 1 Corinthians 7:3–5, 10–16, and Ephesians 5:21–25. What does submission to one another really mean?

10. 1 Peter 3:3–7. What did Simon Peter write about a wife's true beauty? How can wives attain this, and how can husbands help them?

Work—
Labor

Whether we are salespersons or teachers, studying in school, staying home with the children, or climbing telephone poles, we all have the responsibility of work. The Bible challenges us to do something for the betterment of our world as well as for God's glory. Whether we realize it or not, God is working all the time. When some Pharisees criticized Jesus for healing a man on the Sabbath, He said that God is working and that He also works (John 5:17). Jesus is a worker without a hint of laziness. Everyone who is Christ's disciple should be occupied with work. Look at a few Scriptures that challenge us in this area.

1. Genesis 2:15. God created Adam and placed him in the garden of Eden, telling him he had a job to do. Has that order been revoked? How is work a blessing?

2. Nehemiah 4:3–6, 21. The Hebrews had returned from captivity in Babylon. They rebuilt the walls of Jerusalem in fifty-two days. How were they criticized? With what attitude did they work? How can we learn from their work ethic?

3. Proverbs 24:30–34. What happens to people who are lazy and

won't work? What are some ills of society that could be solved by work?

4. Matthew 5:16. Jesus says we should let our light shine. For what purpose? Who receives the praise? How is God glorified through Christians' lives?

5. Romans 16:1. Paul commended Phoebe, a church deaconess. Deacon, *diakanos* in Greek, means "servant." Do you know people who work in your church without calling attention to themselves?

6. 1 Corinthians 3:9. Have you thought of our being God's partners in daily work? What did Paul say about work? Discuss how we work with God.

7. 1 Corinthians 15:56–58. Since a great future awaits God's people, what should be our attitude toward work? Why is work in God's kingdom never in vain or useless?

8. Ephesians 2:8–10. How do we become Christians? If God's grace saves us, why should we work? What does Paul call us? What kind of work should we do?

9. 2 Thessalonians 3:10–13. What does Paul say about those who refuse to work? What is the danger of being idle? What is Paul's final admonition?

10. Hebrews 10:24. What is mentioned before work or good deeds in this verse? How can we encourage others to work? How do we teach children to be responsible? Do you have suggestions for the unemployment problem?

Worship 102

True spiritual worship is the recognition and reverence of God as the Lord of life. We bow down before God, we esteem Him, and we lift up His glorious name, individually and in large or small congregations. In our praying, singing, and work, we should worship the Lord with passion, devotion, and honest daily living. Worship is not a dull, lifeless ritual or routine, but a joyful experience of God's presence.

During Christ's triumphal entry into Jerusalem, the people sang praises and spread palm branches in the path before Him. Some Pharisees told Jesus to stop His disciples from doing this. Jesus said that if His followers were to stop praising Him, the rocks would cry out (Luke 19:39-40 NIV).

However, God does not accept sham worship or vain repetitions. Worship means loving the Lord with our heart, mind, soul, and strength. Consider true worship as a way of life.

1. Exodus 4:29–31. What moved the Israelites to worship the Lord? How can we worship God wherever we are?

2. Job 1:18–20. How did Job respond to the news of the deaths of his children? What attitude should we have toward God in good times and bad? Why?

3. Isaiah 6:1–8. Where was God in Isaiah's vision? What message did the angelic beings express? What initial response did Isaiah make? What did he plead in verse 8?

4. Ezekiel 8:14–16. Some Hebrews worshiped Tammuz, the god of nature. What were the twenty-five men worshiping, their backs to the temple? They made cakes of bread for the pagan Queen of Heaven (Jeremiah 7:18; 44:17–19, 25). What other forms of worship did they practice? Why was this wrong? How did God react?

5. Matthew 2:10–11. Wise men journeyed to Bethlehem after Jesus was born, giving gifts to Jesus at His home, and they worshiped Him. Why do we worship Jesus? (Philippians 2:5–11).

6. Matthew 14:28–33. When Peter called out to the Lord on the water, what did he attempt to do? What distracted him and made him afraid? What did Jesus ask him as He reached out to rescue him? What was the response of the disciples?

7. Matthew 28:16–17. When the disciples met Jesus before His ascension, what did they do? What was the reaction of some? How do we worship the Lord? Your answers will vary.

8. John 4:20–24. What did Jesus teach the woman at the well about worship? What are the two vital elements of worship?

9. Colossians 2:18. Paul warned against the worship of angels. What early tendency did men have with regard to worship? (Romans 1:25). Does this kind of worship continue to this day? Who alone is to be worshiped?

10. Revelation 5:13–14. All creatures in the universe will worship God and the Lamb. The twenty-four elders represent all the redeemed who will worship. Share some worship experiences.

Postlude

When John Wesley was listening to the preface of Martin Luther's commentary on Romans, he said he felt his heart "strangely warmed." As you search through the Scriptures and discuss the questions in this book, or meditate on them at home, I pray that your heart will be strangely warmed, as well. And may these Bible studies help keep Jesus and your relationship to Him the central focus of your life.

For Further Reading

Butler, Trent, general editor. *Holman Illustrated Bible Dictionary*. Nashville: Holman Publishers, 2003. (Any Bible dictionary is a good resource.)

Evans, Morris, managing editor. *International Standard Bible Encyclopedia* (4 volumes). Grand Rapids, MI: Eerdmans, 1956.

Garrett, James Leo. *Systematic Theology*, Vols. 1 & 2. Grand Rapids, MI: Eerdmans, 1990.

Graham, Billy. *Angels*. Waco, TX: Word, 1995.

Halley, H. H. *Halley's Bible Handbook*. Grand Rapids, MI: Zondervan, 1965.

Nave, Orville. *Nave's Topical Bible*. Chicago: Moody Press, 1974.

Thompson, Frank Charles. *Thompson Chain Reference Bible*. Kirkbride Bible Co., 1964. Miracles of the Bible listed with biblical references: Miracles of: Moses, Joshua, Samson, Samuel, Prophets of Judah, Elijah, Elisha, Isaiah, Jesus Christ, Peter, Paul, Disciples of Jesus, 2352–2353.

Trench, Richard C. *Notes on the Miracles of Our Lord*. Grand Rapids, MI: Zondervan, 1951. (Copyright, Baker Book House, 1949.)

About the Author

Preston Taylor was a pastor and missionary to Argentina. He received his BD and ThM degrees from Southwestern Baptist Seminary and his DMin from Luther Rice. For the past twenty-five years, he wrote weekly devotional messages for newspapers in the towns where he served as pastor. Dr. Taylor went home to his Lord while this book was in the process of publication.